A LITTLE BIT

OF

FENG SHUI

A LITTLE BIT
OF
FENG SHUI
AI MATSUI JOHNSON

AN INTRODUCTION TO
THE ENERGY OF THE HOME

STERLING ETHOS

STERLING ETHOS
New York

An Imprint of Sterling Publishing Co., Inc.

ISBN 978-1-4549-4433-1
ISBN 978-1-4549-4434-8 (e-book)

Distributed in Canada by Sterling Publishing Co., Inc.
Canadian Manda Group, 664 Annette Street
Toronto, Ontario M6S 2C8, Canada
Distributed in the United Kingdom by GMC Distribution Services
Castle Place, 166 High Street, Lewes, East Sussex BN7 1XU, England

Distributed in Australia by NewSouth Books
University of New South Wales, Sydney, NSW 2052, Australia
For information about custom editions, special sales, and premium and corporate purchases, please
contact Sterling Special Sales at 800-805-5489 or specialsales@sterlingpublishing.com.

Manufactured in Malaysia

2 4 6 8 10 9 7 5 3 1

sterlingpublishing.com

Cover design by Elizabeth Mihaltse Lindy
Interior Design Gina Bonanno

Getty Images: DigitalVision Vectors/Thoth_Adan: 38;
Stock/Getty Images Plus/Dksamco: 20
Shutterstock.com: Akane1988: 11
Cyril Hou: 13; Polii: 22; sashua d: throughout (baguan);
Kennedy Liggett: 52, 53, 56, 68

CONTENTS

INTRODUCTION

When you hear the words "Feng Shui," what comes to mind first? Some ancient Chinese magic that can change your life drastically? Changing your furniture layout based on the directions of a compass? Cleaning, organizing, and decluttering your home? Possibly you have no idea at all. Feng Shui, a form of ancient Chinese wisdom, may be misunderstood as superstition by people today, but I consider Feng Shui to be a practical and useful art, based on intuition, common sense, logic, and psychological theory, rather than superstition or fortune telling. It is true, however, that Feng Shui is not a science. I am not here to promise that it will necessarily change your life drastically. But I am introducing Feng Shui to you in hopes that its philosophy could benefit you if you are willing to improve your living environment and lifestyle.

Feng Shui is a holistic approach and technique that can open us up to our better being, by balancing "Chi" (energy) between people and the environment. Its theories of Yin and Yang and the Five Elements are used in acupuncture as well, as both are used in Traditional Chinese Medicine.

In chapter 1, you will find out exactly what Feng Shui is. Chapter 2 will delve into Chi energy, how it flows in a space and its cycles, Taoism, Yin Yang Theory, and the Five Elements, which are the basic principles of Feng Shui. In chapter 3, I will provide you with a bit of history of Feng Shui. I will introduce different styles of Feng Shui, from Classic Chinese Feng Shui to a contemporary Feng Shui (Western style, Black Sect Tantric Buddhist Feng Shui, aka BTB), and Chinese astrology in chapter 4. In chapter 5, I will show the basic way to analyze your environment from a Feng Shui perspective. In chapter 6, I will introduce Feng Shui basic placement theory. Then, in chapter 7, you will learn directions, colors, and furniture placement, based on "Bagua"—one of Feng Shui's tools. Chapter 8 will focus on how to implement basic Feng Shui room by room: the entryway, the living room, the bedroom, the kitchen, and the bathroom. In chapter 9, I will talk about how you can apply Feng Shui basics in relationships with your family members, partners, friends, bosses, colleagues, and whomever you interact with in your community, to promote living in harmony. If you want to learn Feng Shui's basic principles and tips quickly, this is the book for you!

Home—the space you live in—reflects who you are, how you view things, how you interact with others, and how you present yourself to the world. Similarly, your working environment (often in an office building or a post-COVID home office) may affect your emotions and thoughts, productivity, creativity, efficiency, and possibly your income. Further, these elements may affect your health as well.

Learned ancient Chinese people knew this, so they used Feng Shui experts to help them and their family receive good fortune that could last for generations.

When I first learned Feng Shui, I was a teenager in Japan, where I was born and raised. I assume that most of the readers of this book are Westerners in English-speaking countries, whose basic culture is different from mine. Therefore, there may be a slight gap between what you think you know about Feng Shui and what I thought about Feng Shui back then.

As a teenager, I enjoyed reading books about Feng Shui and trying out the ideas in my own home. My family used to make fun of me because they did not believe in Feng Shui. Back then, Feng Shui was very big in Japan, and there was a famous Feng Shui master who started a Feng Shui trend in the 1990s. He published a lot of books and he appeared on many TV shows and in many magazines. When he said, "If you want financial luck, put some yellow items in the western part of your house," I (and everybody else) bought something yellow and put it in the western part of our homes. When he said, "If you want to get the right information at the right time, put audio equipment and a TV set in the eastern part of your house," everybody moved their audio equipment and TVs to the eastern side of their homes. I did as well. Even though I was not sure if it was truly effective, I followed his guidance and placed items with certain colors and shapes in certain areas of my house for certain purposes.

But as I grew up, I started wondering . . . "Is this really what Feng Shui is supposed to teach us?" Because if everybody is putting yellow items on the western side of their home for wealth, everybody should become wealthy. Even as a young adult, I already knew life was not that easy.

Before leaving Japan for New York in 2008, I took a Feng Shui Interior Coordinator course and obtained a certification. What I learned from the teacher was not exactly the same as what I had learned about Feng Shui from books before. It was more detailed and deeper than I thought, and many things now made more sense to me. I learned that Feng Shui is not only about colors, shapes, and directions, but that it is a technique that teaches us how to focus on our intentions and show them to the Universe clearly so that it can help us reach our goals.

It took me almost eleven years for me to start working as a professional Feng Shui interior design consultant in New York City after I studied Feng Shui in Japan. I worked at different jobs in various fields, but I must tell you that being a Feng Shui interior design consultant is the most exciting and fulfilling job of my life. I am thrilled to introduce you to the basics of Feng Shui through this book, and I hope that it will stir your interest in Feng Shui so that you start using it in your home on a daily basis, much as you may exercise or meditate every day.

Since this book is an introduction to Feng Shui, the information I share here is very basic and general. Not everything I discuss will apply to you, your home, or your situation. Each of us is different, just as each home is different. Sometimes, Feng Shui rules need to be modified, based on your own personal situation, your family situation, or your home's structure. A Feng Shui remedy that you found on the internet may not work for you and your home. I cannot emphasize enough that a proper Feng Shui adjustment or treatment should be something that is personal and customized. I highly recommend that you consult with a professional Feng Shui expert if you are seeking to apply a Feng Shui treatment for you and your home in a more precise way.

I do not suggest that Feng Shui can cure your health problems, make you wealthy, or bring you your future life partner. What I do suggest, however, is that Feng Shui can be used as a tool to help you to focus your efforts and commitment to help improve your life.

I hope *A Little Bit of Feng Shui* will give you an opportunity to review your living and working environment, your lifestyle, and your relationships so that you may make adjustments here and there to keep them in harmony. Are you ready to begin the Feng Shui lifestyle?

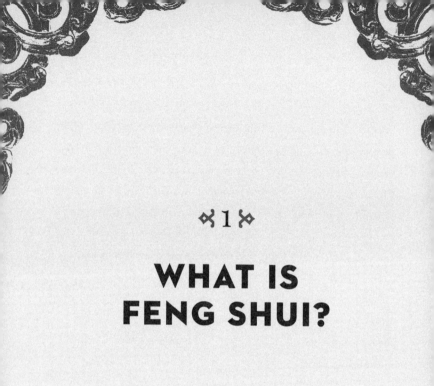

❖ 1 ❖

WHAT IS
FENG SHUI?

F ENG SHUI IS AN ANCIENT CHINESE ART AND PHILOSOPHY
that teaches us how to harmonize *Chi* (energy) in ourselves
with Chi in any given environment: homes, offices, gardens,
restaurants, etc. The purpose of Feng Shui is to connect the two
worlds of Heaven (or the Universe, invisible energy, Father energy,
Yang) and Earth (visible energy, Mother energy, *Yin*), and to keep us
(Humanity) in harmony between these two worlds. This concept is
called *Taoism*—a 6,000-year-old Chinese philosophy, which I will
explore in more detail, along with Yin Yang Theory in a later chapter.
Taoism teaches us oneness through two opposing energies, Yin and
Yang, such as Female/Male, Night/Day, Death/Birth, Shadow/
Light.

Stephen Feuchwang, an emeritus professor of anthropology at
the London School of Economics, referred to Feng Shui this way:

"To be in the right place, facing the right direction, doing the right thing at the right time . . . a cross between being practically efficient and being ritually correct. It is being in tune with nature" (An Anthropological Analysis of Chinese Geomancy [Bangkok: White Lotus Co., 1974]).

In other words, Feng Shui helps us be in the right place, doing the right thing, at the right time, by allowing us to follow the patterns of nature, which helps us achieve our goals in life.

In the literal translation from Chinese, *Feng* (風) is "Wind"; *Shui* (水) is "Water." Wind represents the aspects of our lives that are invisible, such as the air we breathe or the sounds we hear, which can nevertheless be felt. Water represents the aspects of our lives that are visible, such as water itself.

We could also consider *Feng* as the spiritual aspect of our lives and *Shui* as the physical aspect of life. Feng Shui teaches that when we are in harmony, our potential to be successful in all aspects of life is maximized, including our careers, our relationships, our self-development, our health, and our wealth.

Feng Shui consultants must be skilled at reading forms of the land, seasonal patterns, and the rhythms of nature, and they must have a knowledge of colors, shapes, materials, and direction. In ancient China, people used these skills when creating villages, towns, cities, and the layout of the country, with the goal of ensuring the safety of the people and abundant crop harvests. For instance, the ancient Chinese used Feng Shui to select where to plant crops and to select burial sites, because they believed that good or bad Feng Shui, on especially a Royal family's burials, might affect their ancestors' fortunes and possibly the entire nation's future.

You can see the influences of Feng Shui in the design of cemeteries, gardens, temples, and palaces, as well as houses, offices, and restaurants in Hong Kong and China. Other Eastern countries, such as Taiwan, Singapore, Korea, and my home country of Japan, have also been greatly influenced by Feng Shui. In each country, Feng Shui developed in its own unique expression to fit the culture of the countries. Feng Shui practices have developed in Western countries as well, which we will address in greater detail later. No matter which variant of Feng Shui one practices, however, the basic idea is the same: Feng Shui aims to generate and invite positive energy while minimizing negative energy.

Modern Feng Shui practitioners have made certain modifications to traditional Feng Shui practices to facilitate the application of Feng Shui principles to modern Western life. Contemporary Western life is obviously very different from the way people lived in ancient China. In those days in China, people believed that it was best to build their house with a mountain to the north, behind the house, and a river to the south, in front of the house. A practical reason for doing so is that the mountain to the north could protect the home from the cold winds in the winter (as well as the sands and cold winds from Mongolia in the spring), while providing shade in the summer. Meanwhile, having a river to the south let the residents enjoy sunlight and a water view, which they believed brought good luck.

But how realistic is it for most people to situate their homes between a mountain to the north and a river to the south? Further, developments in heating and cooling technologies have made such positioning less consequential. That said, employing the principles of Feng Shui, adjusted to meet the practical needs of modern life, promotes progress toward the same end: inviting positive energy while minimizing negative energy.

Although Feng Shui has become more visible and popular in Western countries in the past few decades, I must emphasize that many of the fundamental concepts and history of Feng Shui have been overlooked in the process. In Western culture, Feng Shui tends to be seen as just another interior decorating approach or decluttering method, but the concept is not that simple. In the next few chapters, I will introduce you to the deeper aspects of Feng Shui—its origin and philosophy—because understanding its roots is important to help guide you in the application of Feng Shui to your life.

What Is Feng Shui?

❖ 2 ❖

WHAT IS "CHI" ENERGY?

To understand Feng Shui and practice it effectively, it is very important for you to understand the concept of *Chi*.

You may have had an experience in which you felt very comfortable spending hours in a restaurant, though normally you would want to leave right after dining. This is because you felt *Chi* in this restaurant. Likewise, you may have been shopping and found that you preferred to buy an item from one sales clerk as opposed to another staff member. This is also because you feel Chi in the first clerk.

Below is the Chinese symbol for Chi, also known as Qi.

In ancient China, people believed that calmly flowing water, such as a river, provided good Chi that could bring them good fortune.

FIGURE 1. CHINESE SYMBOL FOR CHI

Additionally, the Chinese considered mountains or hills as sources of support that could provide security. Therefore, the best way for them to receive positive energy was to live in a house with a river in front and a mountain behind. Palaces, temples, gardens, and houses often had water forms near them, such as a river, an ocean, a lake, a pond, or a fountain. We still see the same thing today throughout the world. It is universal that humans feel pleasant living near the water.

Chi is spelled as Qi (氣) in Chinese, Gi (기) in Korean, and Ki (気) in Japanese. Chi is considered to be a life force—the ability to do work—that flows in our bodies as well as in animals, plants, buildings, sounds, art, and food. Chi is literally in everything. Although we cannot see Chi with our eyes, somehow we can feel it.

Eastern culture highly values Chi and its flow, which is reflected in our customs, behaviors, and even languages. For example, the Japanese language has more than 300 words that contain kanji 気 (ki). The literal translation for 元気 (gen ki) is "original energy," which means good health or spirits. Similarly, 天気 (ten ki) is "heaven's energy," meaning weather. 気に入る(ki ni iru) is "to be in the energy," meaning that I'm pleased with or I like [something]. If Japanese has this many Chi-words, I assume that Chinese has even more. Once I asked my American husband if he could come up with any English idioms that contain the word *energy*; he could not. I would be very curious to know if you could think of any.

In science, energy is a vibration and electromagnetic energy that flows in everything. Cosmic activities—including the movements of planets in the galaxy—affect the surrounding electromagnetic fields, which also affect humans, animals, and plants on Earth. The ancient Chinese, as well as the Greeks, the Egyptians, the Mayans, and the Indians knew this, and used these concepts to develop astrology. Ancient Chinese astrology is one of Feng Shui's components, which I will discuss a bit later.

Chi flows inside of everything as well as on the surface of everything. Chi flows are often compared to water flows. Compare a river that flows fiercely, straight, and fast to a river that flows in a slow and winding fashion. Which is the calming energy? If you are in bed trying to rest, which type of energy would you like to feel? Feng Shui is a technique to create an ideal path for Chi to flow in space. For this purpose, Feng Shui would aim to create the path of the slow and winding river.

Depending on the occasion, season, time, place, purpose, or roles that we play in society, the Chi in ourselves and our environment can change to fit the circumstances. I just suggested that the ideal Chi flow when you are trying to rest is the slow and winding river, a calming, soothing energy. But what if you were watching a boxing match right by the ring with hundreds of people in a crowd around you (imagine this is before COVID) . . . Would you feel this calming energy or the fast, fiercely flowing energy? The latter, right? Sometimes, that is the feeling you want to evoke, and through Feng Shui we can purposely design spaces to let Chi flow as we intend. This is known as mindful design, or environmental design. Modern environmental psychology shares many of these Feng Shui concepts. You can find this type of design anywhere today. A fast food restaurant's interior design is a good example. Many fast food restaurants incorporate "hot" colors, such as red, orange, and yellow. Can you guess why? First, those colors catch our attention immediately, stimulate our senses, and keep us excited—thus subliminally encouraging us to spend money to eat and drink. Second, they do not keep our focus maintained too long. That is to say, these colors do not encourage customers to feel too comfortable and thus spend a long time dining. Such restaurants also often play up-tempo music in the background to foster the same effect. Fast food restaurants want their customers to eat fast and leave, to give them a quick turnover in tables and thus maximize profits. In this context, the customers can be considered as Chi, and their fast turnover is the Chi flow.

The same Feng Shui design strategy would not be applied, for example, in a spa. A spa is a place where customers want to feel relaxed and refreshed, to allow them to enjoy an extended time in a quiet atmosphere, receiving spa treatments. Therefore, the goal for Chi in the spa is very different from that in a fast food restaurant.

There are some different types of Chi. I will introduce three important kinds of Chi for you to recognize: Sheng Chi (生气: positive, growing energy), Sha Chi (煞气: negative, killing energy), and Si Chi (死气: negative, dying energy).

SHENG CHI

Sheng Chi means a "good, positive, bright, uplifting energy." Sheng Chi is also known as the "Happy Dragon's Breath." Feng Shui's goal is to invite positive energy into the house to let us receive as much good luck as possible. Good energy moves in a wavy line at a steady pace. Remember the winding river? That is how good energy flows. Beautiful flowers, plants, water, art, crystals, scents, and sounds can all attract good energy. Further, a mindful interior design and furniture layout can help guide positive energy to travel smoothly in the space, which generates good fortune. You may have noticed that the entryways of Chinese restaurants sometimes have a comforting wind chime, a beautiful flower arrangement, bamboo trees, or a fish tank. Those are all examples of using Feng Shui to attract Sheng Chi.

SHA CHI

Sha Chi means a "bad, negative, attacking energy." Feng Shui attempts to minimize or eliminate this bad energy in the space and keep bad luck out of the house. Sha Chi moves very fast in a straight line. The sharp corners of walls or tables create Sha Chi, which is also called "poison arrow" because it is an attacking energy. Be sure not to have any poison arrows pointing straight toward you when you're sleeping in your bed or while working at your desk, as this could negatively affect your health.

SI CHI

Si Chi is a decaying, lessening, dying energy. It is completely opposite from Sheng Chi. Feng Shui attempts to remove this energy in the space and even prevent its creation. It can be found both inside and outside the house. For example, places where human massacres, natural disasters, or other traumatic incidents occurred have this dying energy. Sick people, sick animals, and dying plants also exude this type of energy. Likewise, keeping a lot of clutter, junk, or unused things in one's house can create such negative energy, as can repressing one's emotions.

The value of banishing such energy was popularized by Marie Kondo, with her "KonMari Method." Her method encourages people to retain items that "spark joy" and get rid of items that carry negative energy. Essentially, she is suggesting that we work to eliminate Si Chi and create spaces that welcome positive energy, or Sheng Chi.

I have seen many Westerners misunderstand that space cleansing (including cleaning, organizing, and decluttering) alone is Feng Shui. Cleansing is something that has to be done in connection with Feng Shui, but in and of itself it is not Feng Shui. Space cleansing alone is not a complete form that brings you good fortune, but it is a primary process that needs to be done as part of a Feng Shui treatment.

Imagine that you did lots of decluttering and your house became almost empty, or that you organized all your clothing into neat, perfectly folded groups so that all your clothes were in their place. This may well make you feel accomplished and refreshed. At that point, however, what you have done is just get rid of unfavorable energy. Next, you have to shape and enhance the energy in your space to attract and welcome positive energy.

Of course, the converse is true as well: You can do Feng Shui in your home perfectly, but if your home remains dirty and filled with clutter, Feng Shui will not work for you. Therefore, Feng Shui and space cleansing must be done together. Remember: The whole point of Feng Shui is to minimize bad energy, maximize good energy, and generate positive energy in the house to live in harmony, so that we can receive good fortune.

How do we do that with Feng Shui? We use Taoism, Yin Yang Theory, and the Five Elements. These three concepts are extremely important in Feng Shui. We will explore these matters next.

TAOISM

Taoism is an ancient Chinese philosophy that teaches us the importance of living in harmony with the Tao. Tao means the "Way" in Chinese, and Tao shows us how to stay in harmony with the physical world (Earth) and the spiritual world (the Universe) to achieve our goals.

The roots of Taoism go back at least to the fourth century BCE. Lao Tzu is regarded as one of the founders of Taoism. Taoism's cosmological concept originated with the School of Yin Yang (or the School of Naturalist), which is a philosophical system that teaches how to keep human behavior in harmony with the cycles of nature.

Yin Yang Theory

Taoism is based on Yin Yang Theory, which was taught by the School of Yin Yang.

FIGURE 2. YIN YANG SYMBOL

You may be familiar with this symbol (see Figure 2). In the circle, you see a white rising part (Heaven, Yang, Masculine energy), which has a small black dot on the top, and you see a black falling part (Earth, Yin, Feminine energy), which has a small white dot on the bottom. This symbol reflects the fact that two opposing energies exist together as a set. One cannot exist without the other; there is no complete Yin or Yang without the other. Each energy contains a little bit of the other. For instance, consider men and women. Men have a feminine side to them, while women have a masculine side.

In Feng Shui consultation, this Yin Yang Theory, along with the Five Elements (which we will discuss later), is used extensively to analyze the energy balance in a space.

Yin Yang Theory reflects bipolar relativity. Fire is generally Yang, but if you were to compare the fire on a candle that is almost extinguished to a campfire that is burning fiercely, the former would be Yin fire while the later is Yang.

THE FIVE ELEMENTS

Each Yin energy and Yang energy can be also categorized as one of five different characteristic elements by Chinese astrology: Wood, Fire, Earth, Metal, and Water. Everything on Earth, including humans, animals, plants, buildings, colors, seasons, and time can be related to one these Five Elements. In Chinese astrology, you may have many of these elements in your astrology chart, since your birth time, day, month, and year are all related to one of these elements. In this book, you can find your Five Elements based on your birth year by using one of the calculation systems, called Kua Number, in the appendix.

WOOD (YANG)

Wood has spring and morning energy, like an uplifting, straight tree growing toward the sky. Wood people are creative, hardworking, goal- and family-oriented, and they enjoy challenges.

COLOR: Green

DIRECTIONS: East, Southeast

FIRE (YANG)

Fire has summer and noon energy; a burning, expanding, exciting, and intense energy. Fire people are energetic, charismatic, dynamic, and influential; they enjoy being in the spotlight.

FIGURE 3. FIVE ELEMENTS CYCLE

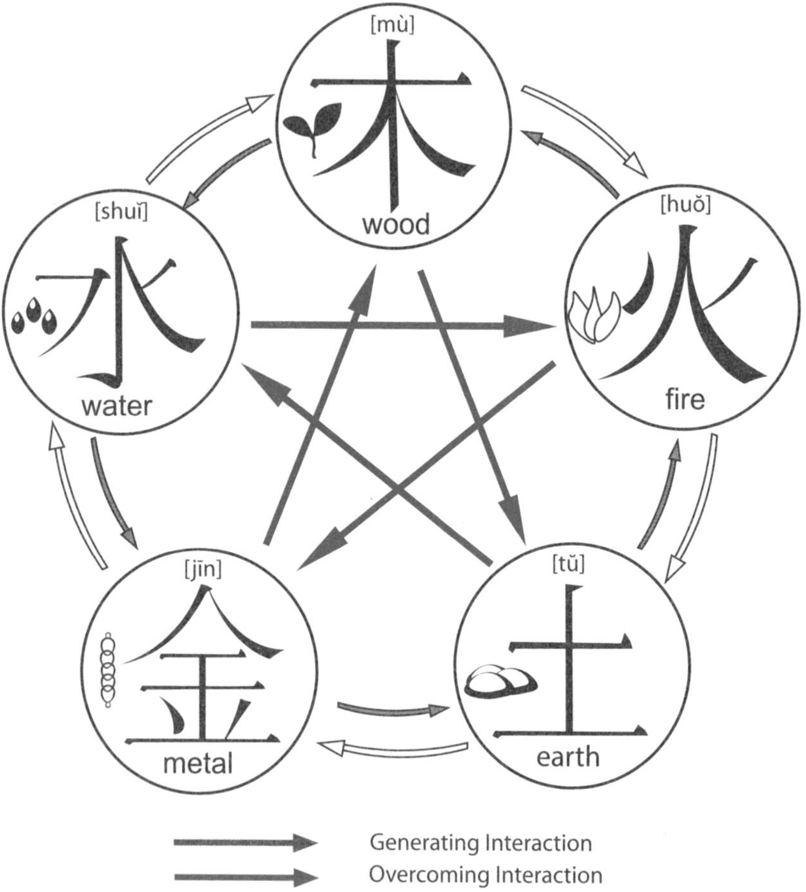

[mù]
木
wood

[huǒ]
火
fire

[shuǐ]
水
water

[jīn]
金
metal

[tǔ]
土
earth

Generating Interaction
Overcoming Interaction

COLOR: Red

DIRECTION: South

EARTH (YIN/YANG)

Earth has late-summer/early-fall and afternoon energy, like the grounding, stabilizing, and nurturing Mother Earth energy. Earth people are reliable, loving, and caring; they enjoy teaching and having responsibility.

COLOR: Yellow

DIRECTIONS: Southwest, Northeast

METAL (YIN)

Metal has late-fall/early-winter and evening/night energy that is condensing, focusing, hardening, and solidifying energy. Metal people are logical, precise, strategic, and tend to be good at finance.

COLOR: White

DIRECTIONS: West, Northwest

WATER (YIN)

Water has winter and midnight energy that is a cooling, flowing, floating, curving, and free energy. Water people are independent, creative, intuitive, and sensitive; they are good at social activity and excellent communicators.

COLOR: Black

DIRECTION: North

Each energy interacts with the others in a creative and controlling way, maintaining harmony (see Figure 3 on page 22). We can observe Yin Yang and Five Element cycles in patterns of nature: seasons, time, and even in human bodies (as taught in Traditional Chinese Medicine, including acupuncture and herbal medicine). We can also find these energies in the interior design of a house or even in people's personalities and relationships.

These Five Elements circulate, which I refer to as "energy flow." I will introduce the most important two ways of circulation: Productive Cycle and Controlling Cycle. Yin Yang Theory, Five Elements, and their cycles are all important to Feng Shui, as well as in Traditional Chinese Medicine.

PRODUCTIVE CYCLE

When the Five Elements cycle goes clockwise, as shown in Figure 3 (with the gray-colored arrows), the cycle is called "Productive Cycle" or "Generating Interaction." Wood feeds Fire, Fire fertilizes Earth (ash, soil), Earth creates Metal (mineral), Metal creates Water, Water nurtures Wood, and so on.

This pattern can be seen in the hours of a day as well as in the seasons of a year. The day begins with morning (Wood), then follows noon (Fire), afternoon (Earth), evening/night (Metal) and midnight (Water), to be followed again by morning (Wood). Likewise, every year, spring comes (Wood), then follows summer

(Fire), fall (Earth), late fall/early winter (Metal), and winter (Water), which, of course, is followed by spring again. This is a natural cosmic order, in which one energy morphs into another, and the cycle repeats itself. Feng Shui recognizes that we feel comfortable in an environment (either in a place or in a relationship) where this productive cycle is functioning smoothly.

CONTROLLING CYCLE

When the Five Elements cycle goes in a pentagram, as shown in Figure 3 on page 22 (with the red arrows), the cycle is called "Controlling Cycle" or "Overcoming Interaction." This cycle does not produce constructive energy; rather, it destroys or cancels other energy. Water extinguishes Fire, Fire melts Metal, Metal chops Wood, Wood exhausts Earth (soil), and Earth dams Water. In this cycle, things don't move forward smoothly.

We feel uncomfortable or weakened, staying in an environment (either in a place or in a relationship) where this controlling cycle is functioning. Sometimes, however, this cycle must happen when one energy is extremely strong, causing negative effects on the others, so it must be dissipated.

Feng Shui's role is to analyze the balance of Yin and Yang, the Five Elements and their cycles in your living and working environment. If the analysis reveals any imbalances, Feng Shui concepts will suggest solutions to create harmony to allow Chi to flow smoothly.

If, however, good balances are already in place, Feng Shui may suggest some enhancements and adjustments to achieve better harmony and Chi flow in order to maximize positive energy.

Your environment reflects your personality, energy, lifestyle, and point of view. As a Feng Shui consultant, I can often identify problems or struggles that my clients have gone through just by observing their space. Sometimes the issue is their health; other times it is their finances or career; still other times it may be their relationship with their family, partner, employer, or a colleague.

For example, I had a client who hired me to improve his apartment and, hopefully, his love life. When I went to his house to analyze the space, believe or not, the area which is considered to be an area for "Love & Relationship" in Feng Shui was extraordinarily cluttered, compared to other areas. In this case, this area was his kitchen, and its windows were covered with piles of old, unused kitchen equipment that he was hoping to use "someday." As a result, he had not even opened his kitchen windows for over eighteen years. Obviously, the energy in his kitchen was stagnant and had collected a lot of Si Chi (negative energy). In Feng Shui, windows represent opportunity and recognition. Even though you may say that you want this or that in your life (which, for him, was the unused kitchen equipment), these items may be blocking opportunities subconsciously, and that obstruction may be reflected in your living environment as it was in his. Together, we freed the Si Chi (negative energy) by removing the clutter and reorganizing the space to allow proper energy flow. How he's doing now? After the consultation, he worked on self-acceptance, rather than clinging to a relationship that did not make him happy, he lost seventeen pounds and got in shape, he found a better job, and he's become happier and healthier.

We will address this more in chapter 9, when I will introduce how we can apply Feng Shui to improve personal relationships and partnerships so that, like my lovelorn client, you, too, can improve your life. Before that, however, I will provide a more in-depth history of Feng Shui in the next chapter.

❖ 3 ❖

HISTORY OF FENG SHUI

THE ORIGINS OF FENG SHUI GO BACK APPROXIMATELY 3,000—4,000 years, in China, though some say even 5,000—6,000 years. There is another theory that the origin of Feng Shui is "Vastu Shastra," which was developed in India around 8,000 years ago. *Vastu Shastra* means "building science" in Sanskrit. Just as with Feng Shui in China, architecture in India has been designed based on Vastu Shastra for many years.

The first documented evidence of Feng Shui practice in China goes back to 618 CE, during the Tang Dynasty. But Feng Shui's fundamental philosophy, Taoism, goes back even further to the fourth century CE.

In ancient times, the Chinese observed the relationship between humans and the environment and found that some surroundings seemed to promote luck, while others had the opposite effect. They learned that mountains, rivers, houses, walls, windows, doors, and the directions they face all had effects on luck in both positive and negative ways. This became the study of Feng Shui, and it came from Taoism and Yin Yang Theory, which I introduced in the previous chapter.

I cannot talk about the history of Feng Shui without mentioning three mythological emperors, known as the Three Sovereigns, who contributed to the development of Feng Shui.

THE THREE SOVEREIGNS

Fu Hsi is the mythological first Emperor of China (2852–2737 BCE). He formulated the concept of Yin and Yang and created the eight trigrams (Bagua), including the *I Ching*, which are used as tools of Feng Shui.

The second Emperor, Shin No, or the "Divine Farmer" in English (2737–2698 BCE), taught basic agriculture to his people, and applied Taoism and Yin and Yang to agricultural technology. Through the process of studying plants and herbs, he deepened his understanding of the seasonal, planetary, and cosmic influences on human life, which became the basis for the ancient systems of astrology and Traditional Chinese Medicine (TCM).

The third Emperor is the Yellow Emperor (2698–2598 BCE), who wrote the *Nei Ching*—his own classic text on internal medicine. This is the oldest Chinese medical book and a fundamental source of TCM. After discovering that certain foods have particular effects on the human body, he applied his studies of energy flow to the body, which eventually became TCM, including acupuncture and herbal medicine.

The *Nei Ching* suggests that people should practice all eight branches of TCM to live healthy, happy, long lives. These are:

1. Acupuncture
2. Herbology
3. Nutrition
4. Meditation
5. Exercise (T'ai chi, Qigong)
6. Bodywork (Tui Na massage)
7. Astrology
8. Feng Shui

As you can see, Feng Shui is not an isolated subject, but part of TCM. Thus, Feng Shui is not just another approach to interior design, but rather a philosophical touchstone that the Chinese have developed over thousands of years.

Many buildings and cities in China have been constructed using the principles of Feng Shui throughout its long history.

One of the best examples is the Forbidden City in Beijin, which was constructed during the Ming Dynasty (1407–1420 CE). The Forbidden City was built on 178 acres (72 hectares of land) as a residential pavilion of the Emperor Yong Le, when he decided to move a capital from Nanjin to Beijin. His motivation behind creating the Forbidden City was that it allowed him to occupy the most powerful command position available against the rising threat posed by Mongolia. Following the ancient Chinese Feng Shui principle, the buildings in the Forbidden City were arranged to face south toward water and in front of hills to the north (he even had artificial hills constructed!). This city was considered to have a perfect Yin and Yang balance because this was a powerful layout for the Emperor.

FENG SHUI IN THE WEST

Now let us see how Feng Shui was introduced to Western countries. Contemporary Feng Shui, known as BTB (Black Sect Tantric Buddhist), which has been widely popular in the Western world, was developed by Thomas Lin Yun in the 1970s. He was a Black Sect Tantric Buddhist (Tibetan Buddhist) from Taiwan, and a professor at the University of California in Berkeley, as well as other academic institutions all over the world. After he introduced BTB to the United States, it started to become popular in the mid-1980s. He combined ancient Chinese philosophy with Tibetan Buddhism, and applied it to Feng Shui with some simplified methods that fit the modern lifestyle in Western society, so that more people could be comfortable using Feng Shui. As you already learned in chapter 2, traditional Feng Shui's underlying philosophy is Taoism, which is often confused with Buddhism, but they are two different things. Lin Yun established the Temple in Berkeley, in 1986, devoted his life to serving as a bridge between the East and the West, and passed away in 2010. BTB incorporates the spiritual essences of Tibetan Buddhism: rituals, ceremonies, remedies, transcendental cures, and meditations. This may be why Feng Shui in Western countries tends to be considered a more spiritually oriented subject than a realistic, logical practice, based on ancient Chinese philosophy.

Some classically trained Feng Shui experts don't consider BTB to be real Feng Shui. Their concern is that much of the philosophy, history, and fundamental techniques of Feng Shui have been lost in translation in the Western countries. One of my intentions in writing the first five chapters, including this chapter, is to introduce the overlooked essences of Feng Shui, and evoke interest in Feng Shui's original concept and history, before jumping into how it's used. I am not trying to convince you to believe in only Classic Feng Shui, though. As a Feng Shui consultant who uses both styles, I understand the pros and cons of both. Personally, I think that this type of argument is similar to someone saying, "Only classical music is real music, and other music, like jazz and rock, is not." Music and sound are energy, and there are many different ways to form certain sounds and rhythms as well as techniques to express them. Whatever genre of music you play or listen to, in the end, what matters is whether you feel good. Right? And knowing classical music, its theory and origins may give you more joy regardless of what other genre of music you are into. Similarly, no matter what style of Feng Shui you use—whether it's Classic Feng Shui or BTB—I want you to remember that the purpose of Feng Shui is the same: It will help you learn how to harmonize energy within an environment, analyze its flow and cycle, and maximize positive energy to welcome good fortune while minimizing negative energy.

I will focus on different styles of Feng Shui in the following chapter.

❖ 4 ❖

STYLES OF
FENG SHUI

THE FENG SHUI STYLE THAT IS BEST KNOWN IN ASIAN COUN-
tries follows the Classic Chinese Feng Shui, which is a
combination of the Form School and the Compass School.
Western-style Feng Shui (BTB, Black Sect Tantric Buddhist), which
I mentioned in the last chapter, does not require a compass, unlike
Classic Chinese Feng Shui, and because of its simplified technique
and its spiritual aspects, many Western people enjoy using it.

The Form School (the oldest school) is physical and incorporates
geology to relate to our senses as well as our intuition. This school's
focus is on the influences of geological formations and the shape of
the landscape.

Traditionally, there are four symbolic animals associated with
the four directions and colors used in the Form School. These four
are mythological creatures that appear in the Chinese constellations
along the ecliptic (the plane of the Earth's orbit around the Sun), and
are regarded as the guardians of the four cardinal directions:

- The Black Tortoise to the North (or the back of the house, if you're looking out from inside the house)

- The Red Phoenix to the South (the front of the house)

- The White Tiger to the West (the right side of the house)

- The Green Dragon to the East (the left side of the house)

In modern life, regardless of direction, Black Tortoise may be tall trees or tall buildings behind the house, instead of mountains. Red Phoenix may be a beautiful open view, preferably a water view, a nice park, or a clean street in front of the house. White Tiger may be flower gardens on the right side of the house, and Green Dragon may be tall trees or a building on the left side of the house.

Basic furniture placement can be determined mostly by the Form School as well. For example, when building a house, we avoid placing a bedroom right next to the entrance; rather, it is located far away from it, toward the back of the home. The entrance area is very close to the outer world, where people come in and out, so it is not an appropriate location for the bedroom. In the bedroom, the Form School encourages us to avoid placing the bed close to the bedroom door because the entry is a busy area where energy comes in and out.

THE COMPASS SCHOOL

The Compass School uses tools such as a compass (traditionally, a *Luo Pan compass*) and *Bagua* ("eight areas" in English translation), which is considered as an energy map that consists of eight trigrams, each with three Yin Yang–broken and solid lines, which are parts of the *I Ching*, to determine the Feng Shui analysis (see Figure 4 on page 38).

The Compass School often combines Feng Shui analysis with various Chinese astrological systems. Here are a few of them.

Ming Gua and Ba Zhai

The Ming Gua (Life Destiny) determines a person's lucky directions, colors, items, materials, as well as the unlucky ones, based on their birth year (see the appendix). This system categorizes people into two groups: the East Group and the West Group, which can teach you the compatibility between you and your family or the partner with whom you live. You can also know your home's character by using Ba Zhai (Eight Houses/Mansions). This assesses the compatibility between your personal energy and the home's energy.

Flying Star

Flying Star determines fortune over time and predicts the future. The Flying Star involves time cycles and space that are mapped onto the Bagua. This is considered one of the most powerful techniques in Feng Shui, but it also relies on a very complex system. Thus, it requires years of training to put into practice.

Four Pillars (Ba-Zi)

The Four Pillars is used by Feng Shui experts in China, Hong Kong,

Taiwan, Korea, and Japan. It is an ancient Chinese astrological system that reveals an individual's destiny, based on the hour, day, month, and year of that individual's birth.

The complexity and conflicting information involved in these different astrological systems may be one of the reasons that people find Feng Shui very confusing and difficult to practice.

FIGURE 4. BTB FENG SHUI

A LITTLE BIT OF FENG SHUI

WEALTH + PROSPERITY SE or Rear Left Blue Wood Element	FAME + REPUTATION S or R Middle Red Fire Element	RELATIONSHIPS SW or Rear Right Pink Earth Element
FAMILY E or Middle Left Green Wood Element	HEALTH (Middle) Yellow, Earth Tones	CHILDREN + CREATIVITY W or Middle Right White Metal Element
KNOWLEDGE + SELF-CULTIVATION NE or Front Left Blue Earth Element	CAREER N or Front Middle Black Water Element	TRAVEL + HELPFUL PEOPLE NW or Front Right Gray Metal Element

FIGURE 5. BTB'S BAGUA

Western Style (BTB, Black Sect Tantric Buddhist)

This is the style of Feng Shui that is practiced by most in the West. This simplified style does not require a compass, which means that directions are not taken into consideration. It is also known as "Three Gate Feng Shui," in which the front door of the house or apartment is aligned with one of the bottom three sections of the Bagua (the eight areas). Unlike the Compass School's Bagua, BTB's Bagua is just a square that consists of nine grids (with the center counting as one area, making nine; see Figure 5).

❈ 5 ❈

FENG SHUI ANALYSIS

A CCORDING TO FORM SCHOOL FENG SHUI, THERE ARE certain places that you may want to avoid building a new house or purchasing a home. Basically, Feng Shui principles—drawing on Yin Yang Theory—consider anything too extremely Yin or Yang as an unfavorable Feng Shui. To assess this, in Feng Shui analysis, we apply common sense, logic, and psychological insights as well.

The Yin quality is described using adjectives such as *dark*, *small*, *narrow*, *low*, *dumpy*, *cold*, and *hidden*. Yang adjectives include *bright*, *big*, *wide*, *high*, *dry*, *hot*, and *open*. We do not want to live in a house that is characterized by too much Yin or too much Yang: too dark or too bright, too small or too big, too cold or too hot. To attain the desired outcome, we seek a balance between Yin and Yang.

By applying your intuition and common sense, you may conduct a Feng Shui analysis of your living environment and assess the balance between Yin and Yang in your home, the design of the home's interior and exterior, and the general feel of your neighborhood. Take a moment to examine the environment in which your home is situated. Do you have an open view from the entrance of your house or apartment building? Do you see a busy street? Maybe a beautiful garden or other people's homes? If so, are the homes you see attractive or in disrepair? Do you receive enough sunlight?

If you are living on a noisy, busy street in a city where there are many bars, restaurants, and people out and about, cars and trains are running by, and lights are on all night, your home will be very Yang. You may want to create an appropriate Yin and Yang balance in your home by making it a quiet and cozy place with slightly more Yin vibes (such as earthy color schemes, natural interior design, plants, soft light, quiet music), rather than emphasizing the Yang vibes (vivid color schemes, bold interior design, flashy lighting, loud music). If you have too much Yang environment both inside and outside your home, you may come to feel burned out. On the other hand, if your home is in a basement, has little sunlight or fresh air, is small, dark, cluttered, and wet, you live in an extremely Yin home. You should do your best to make it balanced as much as possible by adding more lighting, a fan to circulate the air, and brighter colors in the interior to bring in more Yang. Living in a home with too much Yin influence may eventually make you feel depressed and could cause other health issues.

You may, however, prefer to feel the same energy level inside and outside your home, with either strong Yang (or Yin) vibes.

There is nothing wrong with that, as long as it fits well with your energy. Feng Shui consultants would never force you to live in a certain environment against your will. We analyze energy in a space and suggest a plan to bring greater harmony into your home so that you can receive more luck—it is all up to you whether to take our advice or not.

A major metropolis like New York City, where I live, is considered to be much more Yang, compared to smaller cities. People with Yang personalities—active, busy, spontaneous, and outspoken—tend to enjoy living in a bigger city, as their energy may go well with the city's energy most of the time. Sometimes, however, city dwellers want to get out a bit and travel somewhere they can enjoy openness, nature, and silence. That's how we try to balance Yin and Yang energy in ourselves, whether knowingly or unknowingly. You may feel more comfortable living in a smaller town, surrounded by nature, rather than a big city, though sometimes you may travel to a big city to enjoy its energetic vibes. It depends on how your own energy harmonizes with a particular surrounding. Whatever living environment you find yourself in now, you should pay close attention to the energy in yourself and see if it is in balance with the energy of the environment. If you seek more balance and harmony, then that is the time to use Feng Shui and Yin Yang Theory. You will learn more about using them in a practical fashion in the next chapter.

Here are a few examples of signs of various Yin and Yang qualities to help you assess the Feng Shui in and around your home.

YIN ENVIRONMENTS

• You live by a cemetery. In Feng Shui, the dead are considered Yin, so living close to a cemetery may be considered to be unfavorable Feng Shui (Si Chi). But even if you do live near a cemetery, if the view from your home is a nice park with beautiful flower gardens, it's not necessarily Yin; it might even be Yang.

• You live by a hospital. Sick people are considered Yin.

• You live by a refuse disposal facility. Garbage and dumps have Si Chi.

• You live by a prison, a jail, or a police station. Those places are tied to criminal activities, and their energy tends to be dark and sharp (Sha Chi).

• You live on a dead end of your street at the bottom of a steep slope. Chi travels fast and runs straight toward your home, which is considered to be Sha Chi.

• A nearby building's sharp corner is pointing toward your home. This also brings attacking energy (Sha Chi).

YIN HOME

• Low ceiling, small, little sunlight because there are few windows or small windows, dark colors, cluttered, dirty (could be a basement apartment).

• The house, apartment building, or unit is an irregular shape.

• There is a downhill slope behind the house (in Feng Shui, we call this "Weak Tortoise").

• The house has some tragic history.

YANG ENVIRONMENTS

- You live near a large park with beautiful trees and flowers. Healthy plants have an uplifting, positive energy (Sheng Chi).

- You live near the ocean, a river, a beautiful lake, or a fountain. As I mentioned, water carries positive energy that Feng Shui suggests can bring us wealth and luck. If the water is stagnant or dirty, however, that makes for bad Feng Shui.

- The neighboring buildings or houses are not too tall so that they do not block views and sunlight from your house.

- No surrounding building has a sharp corner pointing toward your home.

YANG HOME

- High ceilings, spacious, plenty of sunlight with many large windows, bright colors.

- The house, apartment building, or unit is designed in a regular shape—square, rectangular, round, octagonal.

- There is a nice open view from the front of the house.

- There is a hill, mountains, a sturdy fence, or a tall building to the rear of the house (in Feng Shui, we call this "Strong Tortoise").

Note that a home with too many Yang qualities is not considered favorable from a Feng Shui perspective. This might include a house that is constantly exposed to direct sunlight, or a skyscraper or beach house with nearly all glass exterior walls.

YIN YANG ADJUSTMENT

If you determine that you live in a Yin surrounding environment or a Yin home, no need to worry; you do not need to move. There are many things you can do to bring your home into balance through Yin Yang Theory. If your house is next to a cemetery, for example, you could build a tall fence or plant tall trees between your house and the cemetery. Inside the home, you could use bright color schemes and be sure to have plenty of light to bring in Yang energy.

If you live in a Yang home, such as in a skyscraper, the higher the floor on which you live, the more Yang and the less Yin the home has. This means you tend to lack grounding energy. Thus, you may want to bring more Yin, down-to-earth vibes into your home by using earthy color schemes, installing a rheostat or other dimming function for your lighting, and appropriate window treatments, such as curtains or blinds, to limit the amount of direct sunlight.

Observing the environment surrounding your house or building is very important because it gives you an idea of what vibes or energy you should create inside your home to reach a balance. When you walk outside, for example, do you see any trees near your home? Are they blocking the light at the front door of the house? Do they look healthy or unhealthy? Are there any overgrown weeds around? Do you see garbage on the street near your house? Are the traffic patterns going away from the property or coming toward it? As you continue to do this exercise, your ability to analyze your environment and the surrounding energy will gradually be strengthened.

It is almost impossible for us to change the surrounding environment. We may have to live with a view of the parking lot in front of our house or a neighbor's tree blocking our view. What I want to emphasize here is that, even though you may find an unfavorable Feng Shui situation around your home that you have no control over, you can still create a positive environment inside your home by maximizing the good energy while minimizing the bad. You may think that there are too many limitations because you rent an apartment, you do not know how long you will live there, or you have kids who clutter up the house with their toys. But in spite of all that, there are many things you can do to improve the energy in your home. If painting the walls is not allowed, you could consider hanging art on the wall. If hanging art is not feasible, you can place some nice flowers or plants around instead. If you do not like having plants inside the house because you worry about your cat eating them and getting ill, then at least keep the house clean and tidy. If your kids' toys are scattered all over the living room, making you feel "What's the point of practicing Feng Shui in this cluttered room anyway?" then it would be a great time for you to see if you are giving your children too many toys, or maybe you could encourage your kids to put their toys in a box every time they finish playing with them. Do they have an accessible place to store their toys?

While many things are beyond our control in our lives, there are many things that we can control in our homes. Things inside the home are manageable if we intend to do so, if we are creative, and if we have the will to create good energy at home. In my practice, I work with my clients to suggest ideas and how to implement them for better Feng Shui in their home or business. I continue to consult with these clients while they themselves do the work of implementation. I have found that this experience often provides them with an improved lifestyle, career, and relationships, and better self-image and self-esteem. In the early phase of such a project, after observing and evaluating their living situations, clients begin to become more aware of themselves, their needs, their goals, and possibly suppressed emotions or old patterns that are blocking their potential. This is most common when the client is in a space-clearing phase—cleaning, decluttering, and organizing. In taking on this work and awareness, they may bring to the surface something they subconsciously did not want to think about, such as a family problem that had been ignored or a toxic relationship they felt they could not end.

Positive change, however, is already happening to them when they face their reality and make a commitment to bring positive change into their life. After clearing the space, they may have more clarity about their priorities in life and start gaining confidence, self-acceptance, and, finally, self-love.

In the next phase, clients implement a Feng Shui arrangement. This may involve relocating furniture and/or painting walls with more uplifting colors, making the project more challenging, especially for those who live with a partner or family. There may be disagreements about selecting colors, plants, rugs, and so forth. But through communicating and determining their needs or their family's needs, the client can start building confidence and a stronger connection with their partner, family, or roommates. Many of my clients who live with a partner or family told me that their connections became much stronger and more positive during the Feng Shui process. Other clients who live by themselves told me that investing a great deal of time and energy on the home project led them to discover a deeper love of their space and themselves.

Working on a home is a lot of work, and it requires you to spend a lot of positive and powerful energy on yourself. Taking care of your home, cleaning it, maintaining it, and improving it are all actions that come from self-love. This is the reason I made my business motto "Love your home, love yourself." Your intention to improve your living situation is a powerful positive energy that you can tap into when you love yourself. It is almost as if you yourself become Sheng Chi (positive energy) that flows in the space! Your Sheng Chi can also flow to other people around you, and more Sheng Chi can be generated around you. It is indeed a powerful manifestation that you show to the Universe. As a Feng Shui consultant, seeing my clients' powerful positive transformations during the process is the best reward. I have never had any client who did not feel an improvement in their life after completing their Feng Shui project.

In the next chapter, you will learn how to create good energy and prevent the formation of bad energy at home by employing some specific, basic Feng Shui techniques.

FENG SHUI PLACEMENT/ LAYOUT & SOLUTION

FROM THIS CHAPTER ON, WE WILL GRADUALLY SHIFT TO THE more fun, practical aspects of Feng Shui, which I believe you have been waiting for! Sometimes I call Feng Shui "Fun Shui," because once you have learned the principles of Feng Shui, you can apply them to your environment in creative ways, which I find quite enjoyable.

You may already know that there are certain furniture placements that Feng Shui suggests you use, and others to avoid. Most of this theory comes from the Form School, which I discussed in chapter 5. Although not all placement issues will be applicable to your lifestyle or your home structure, it is still good to know the basics of furniture placement, as it is useful in both your home and your workplace. Here I will provide some examples of favorable and unfavorable Feng Shui placement. I also introduce examples of Feng Shui solutions for unfavorable furniture placements that cannot be changed, or certain room features that foster bad Feng Shui.

COMMAND / POWER POSITION: This is one of the best-known Feng Shui placements. To set up 6 command position, locate your furniture—such as a desk, bed, or sofa—so that you can view the entryway and have a solid wall behind you (see Figures 6 and 7). For example, when you place a desk in your office, try to place the desk so that it faces the entry to the room. This allows you to see who is coming into the room and the activity nearby. Feng Shui suggests that this is the most ideal layout for an office, because, in that environment, it is important to establish the command or power energy. In a home office, however, if this is not possible, don't be too concerned. This is your home, and generally strangers don't burst into your home, right? In a business environment, however, including a professional office, a store, or a restaurant, workers should face toward the entry, to be aware of their surroundings and be ready to welcome visitors.

FIGURE 6. COMMAND POSITION FOR THE BED

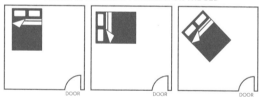

PLACING A PAIR OF ITEMS SYMMETRICALLY: This is also a very well-known Feng Shui placement technique, which is often used in bedrooms. In Feng Shui, it is considered good to locate a bed so that there is an equal amount of empty space on each side of the bed. Also, Feng Shui suggests placing a night table on each side of the bed

FIGURE 7. COMMAND POSITION FOR THE DESK

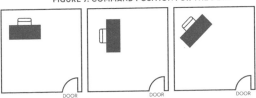

with a lamp on each one (picture the layout of a typical hotel room). Also, you may wish to place two (or four) pillows on the bed, even if you are single. This placement is symbolic, as it shows the Universe that you are ready to be in a relationship by providing a space for someone to come into your life. Maybe, however, you will not be able to place the bed with equal space on both sides because of limited space or the structure of your room. You might need to locate the bed with one side against the wall to save space. If so, that's not the end of the world. As you will see later in this chapter, there are other things you can do to balance the energy of the room. One thing to avoid in Feng Shui for the bedroom: Be sure not to store things under the bed, as this will create stagnated Chi.

CURVY / ZIGZAG LINES IN THE LAYOUT: If more than two doors, windows, or other passageways are set in a straight line, Chi will travel very fast and will create Sha Chi. For example, if you have a door, window, or stairs in front of the main entry, energy will run from the entry through the aligned door, window, or stairs quickly. We seek to avoid this in Feng Shui. To prevent it, you should make a winding path for energy to follow (just like a winding river), with items to interrupt the flow, such as furniture, plants, art, a mirror, or a room divider.

EXAMPLES OF UNFAVORABLE FENG SHUI PLACEMENT/LAYOUT

OTHER ALIGNED DOORS / WINDOWS: If the bathroom door is aligned with any other doors of the house (especially the main entry door), this is bad, because Chi runs into the bathroom and is drained by the Water energy of the bathroom. If you have this layout and often keep the bathroom door and toilet lid open, the first thing you could do to improve the energy of the room is keep them closed. You could also consider hanging a small crystal ball (1.5 inch [40 mm] in diameter or smaller), traditionally with a red string (9, 18, or 27 inches [23 cm, 46 cm, or 69 cm] in length), from the ceiling between the entry door and the bathroom door, because Feng Shui teaches that crystals can disperse energy.

Likewise, the entry to the kitchen should not be aligned with the main entrance door, because Chi will run straight into the kitchen and be burned by the Fire energy of the stove, especially if the stove faces the entry. One solution is to hang a Japanese *noren* curtain or a beaded curtain in the kitchen entry, which will hide the view of the kitchen from the entrance as well as break up the flow of Chi.

It is very common to see home layouts in which the stairs are located directly in front of the main entrance. This is considered bad Feng Shui because the Chi rushes up the stairs without going to the first floor, when ideally it would travel to both floors equally. One easy Feng Shui solution for this is to try to guide Chi into the first floor by placing a beautiful flower arrangement or green plants on a table by the stairs.

DARK, NARROW, LONG, AND STRAIGHT HALLWAY: Chi can turn into Sha

Chi when it runs through a dark, narrow, long, and straight hallway. To make Chi travel in a winding fashion, the easiest thing to do with Feng Shui is to hang art on the walls in a way that creates a zigzag line. Another easy solution is to place a runner or rugs on the hallway floor. Of course, you can combine these two techniques as well. Finally, good lighting in a hallway helps provide a Yang quality.

MISSING CORNER: Ideal Feng Shui suggests certain shapes for houses and other buildings: square, rectangular, or hexagonal. In practice, we see many irregular shapes in modern houses or apartments, which can create what we call a "missing corner" or a "missing area." This means that some of the eight aspects of your life, shown in Bagua (see chapter 7), are lacking—that's why it's called the "missing corner." One example is an L-shaped house or apartment. Although it is usually impossible to change the structure of a house or a building, there are several things you can do to address the missing corner with Feng Shui. For example, if you own your home, and the house has a missing corner, you could fill it by creating a garden outside, to make it feel as though the shape of the house were rectangular. If you live in an apartment with a missing corner, one Feng Shui technique you may want to try is to hang a mirror on either one of the walls facing where the missing corner would be. The reflection of the room in the mirror creates an illusion that there is more space (see Figure 8).

POISON ARROW: Any sharp corner of a piece of furniture or a home's structure can form unfavorable Chi, which is called "Poison Arrow"—a negative, attacking energy. It can be treated by placing

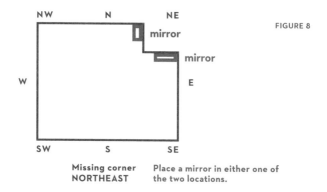

FIGURE 8

Missing corner
NORTHEAST

Place a mirror in either one of
the two locations.

plants in the area or hanging a crystal ball from the ceiling. Another simple way is to change the layout of the furniture to avoid the issue.

BAD BEDROOM LAYOUTS: When the bed (either the foot or head) is aligned with the entry, a window, the bathroom door, or a mirror facing the bed, this is one of the worst bedroom layouts. Why? The energy that comes in and out of the door or window will disturb your sleep. The same is true of having a mirror facing the bed. Most of my clients who have sleeping issues have arranged their bedroom in one of these fashions. Simply changing the layout or removing the mirror often improves the quality of their sleep. If changing the layout is not feasible, hanging a crystal ball between the bed and the door or window can break up the energy flow. Similarly, shutting the door, window, and curtains at night will have the same effect.

EXAMPLES OF FENG SHUI SOLUTIONS AND ENERGY ENHANCERS

None of us live in a 100 percent perfect Feng Shui home. There are always problems, but, at the same time, there are always solutions.

Here are some common Feng Shui treatments that you can easily apply in your own home. You may already have a number of the items discussed, so try to use what you have first before purchasing something new. Many Feng Shui arrangements can be done without buying new things, because Feng Shui's focus is not decoration, but rather being selective in what you bring into your home. Feng Shui encourages you to eliminate whatever you are keeping that doesn't serve you functionally or emotionally anymore. It teaches you to keep an auspicious layout that creates a good energy flow in your space.

Now I will introduce Feng Shui solutions that can treat problems by enhancing your space. Most of the items I mention here are things you may already have on hand, but some are items that may be unfamiliar and new. Remember, though: You do not need to do all the Feng Shui treatments at once. Start with something simple, relatable, or whatever makes sense to you first, and, little by little, see how you feel.

Space Clearing

Even though cleaning, decluttering, and organizing are not subjects of Classic Feng Shui, in contemporary practice they have been widely used as part of a Feng Shui solution by many BTB and Classic Feng Shui consultants. Clean, clutter-free, and tidy spaces definitely support better Chi flow.

A spiritual ritual, as BTB Feng Shui practitioners suggest, can also be effective in clearing the energy in a space. This may include the practice of sage burning and playing the rims of "singing" bowls.

Color

Colors are the easiest Feng Shui solutions to apply to enhance the energy in a space and bring in any of the Five Elements. For example, if you want to boost your reputation energy for your work, add some red color as an accent in Reputation Gua in Bagua, which is in the southern part of the house. (You will be introduced to BTB Bagua, the energy map, in depth in chapter 7.) You can use color by painting walls or adding rugs, curtains, accent pillows, or framed art. Be mindful, however, not to use only one color for everything; that would throw off the balance. Balance is the most important factor in Feng Shui.

Plants and Flowers

Healthy plants are great Feng Shui solutions that can address multiple Feng Shui issues. They will create clean air, release oxygen, and infuse positive energy into a space. Plants can help us develop the nurturing and caring part of ourselves, and the green color of a healthy plant's leaves is very soothing. Plants always provide uplifting energy to a space, so it is nice to have them in the entrance hall to welcome guests.

Flowers are also wonderful Feng Shui items. Some people may hesitate to buy fresh-cut flowers because they will die in a week or so. While cut flowers in a vase do not last as long as plants or flowers in soil, their energy is very powerful, and, when fresh, will create positive energy in a space.

Place plants or flowers in the corner of a room that tends to collect and deflect negative Chi. Covering a poison arrow "Sha Chi" created by a sharp corner of a piece of furniture or a wall is also a good Feng Shui solution. Bamboo trees are very popular in urban restaurants and hotels, as they are easy to maintain, very strong, grow quickly, and are resilient. They can be employed in your home to great effect. Bamboo is a symbol of strength, good luck, positive energy, and long life.

Mirrors

Mirrors can make a small area look doubly spacious by reflecting the room. As I mentioned before, you can use a mirror to treat a missing corner by visually pushing back the wall. A mirror can also be helpful when you cannot see things (such as who is entering a room) behind you.

Mirrors can be powerful Feng Shui solutions; however, if you use them in a wrong way, they can cause a problem. Be mindful of what the mirror is reflecting, and make sure it's a positive view. Also, do not hang a mirror in front of the main door, as it pushes back good energy. Finally, do not place two mirrors facing each other across a space, as this creates an energy trap.

Water

Water, particularly moving water, is a very powerful Feng Shui solution. Placing a fish tank, a small fountain, or even art depicting a waterfall or a river can draw energy into a space. Moving water is known for stimulating wealth energy.

Career Gua, Family Gua, or Prosperity Gua on Bagua, or North, East, and Southeast of the house (see page 66) are the best locations in which to place water items. Be sure that the water is always clear and fresh, since dirty or stagnant water can be poisonous for Chi.

Light

Light can eliminate dark, negative energy, which tends to be found in the dusty corners of a room. Light can create uplifting Yang energy in a space quickly. It can also increase energy overall. At night in the bedroom, dimmer light can enhance the romantic mood.

Candles

Candles can also work effectively to eliminate negative energy. You may place a candle in Knowledge Gua on Bagua or Northeast of the house (see page 66) when you do meditation; this can help you connect with yourself.

Art

Paintings, photos, sculpture, stained glass, pottery, and the like can embody Chi, invoking your desire. For example, you can hang a framed piece of art showing lovers in Love & Relationship Gua or the Southwest of the house (see page 66), rather than a picture of a single person, if you are looking to cultivate a romantic relationship.

Art can also fill any missing Five Elements in the area. For instance, if there is a missing corner in Prosperity Gua on Bagua or the Southeast part of the house (see page 66), a picture of trees and a waterfall could be added to fill the missing space.

Sound

Beautiful sound can generate and move Chi. One of the easiest sound items to introduce to your home is a wind chime. The wind chime can also be a good solution for aligned doors. You can hang a wind chime made of metal if you want to bring the Metal element into a space, or hang a wooden wind chime if you seek to introduce a Wood element into a space. These chimes can be hung outdoors or even indoors; for instance, they can be affixed to the inside of the main entrance.

Scent

The appealing scent of fresh flowers, essential oils, incense, and candles can also bring good Feng Shui. It can create a certain mood and increase your energy.

Crystal Balls

Crystal balls are one of the simplest solutions that can be used in many problematic Feng Shui layouts. They can disperse, expand, and transform Chi.

You can hang a crystal ball near a missing corner, between aligned doors, to avoid Sha Chi, or in a bathroom to avoid draining energy in the bathroom. You can also hang a crystal ball in a long, dark, narrow hallway to slow down Chi flow and prevent Chi from morphing into Sha Chi.

Crystal balls can be used as an energy enhancer as well. You can hang one above your head from the ceiling at your work desk, which can give you positive energy that can support your focus.

BTB Feng Shui consultants traditionally hang crystals with a red thread that is 9, 18, or 27 inches (23 cm, 46 cm, or 69 cm) long. Why? These imperial measurements are multiples of nine, and the number nine is considered to hold the most powerful Yang energy in Feng Shui.

Chinese Coins

Chinese coins are round and often have square holes in the middle. This combination of a round and square shape is a symbol of good fortune and wealth. The circular shape represents Heaven (Spirituality, Masculine/Father energy), while the square represents Earth (Materialism, Feminine/Mother energy). When these two energies are in harmony, abundance and wealth (Humanity, Child) will be created. These coins are also used in *I Ching* readings. The most popular way to use these coins to generate good fortune with money is by hanging three, six, or nine coins, tied together with a red ribbon or string, in a straight line on the wall. They may also be placed on a table, in the Prosperity Gua, which is the Southeast portion of the house (see Bagua on page 66). A contemporary Feng Shui technique that was inspired by Chinese coins is to put a square coffee table on a round rug.

Red Envelopes

Traditionally, putting coins and money inside a red envelope is believed to amplify the wealth of both the giver and the receiver. Some Feng Shui consultants prefer to receive payment from their clients in red envelopes, since that is a way to honor the transferring of Feng Shui knowledge. Red is considered the most powerful and the luckiest color in China, which is why red is often used in Chinese New Year celebrations, weddings, and other festivities in China.

The last few Feng Shui items may not seem rational to you, because they arose out of traditional Chinese customs. That said, if you are open and curious enough to try them out and enjoy the process, that can be your Fun Shui.

I have not attempted to list all Feng Shui solutions here, but I am trying to inspire you to use these tips, as well as your own intuition, to find other solutions. I believe that we all have the means to generate positive energy, and trying things out in this way will improve ourselves and our lifestyles. That is, I believe, good Feng Shui.

HOW TO READ AND USE BAGUA, THE ENERGY MAP

FENG SHUI CONSIDERS MANY FACTORS, SUCH AS DIRECTIONS, colors, shapes, textures, materials, numbers, seasons, times, food, and parts of the human body. Because Feng Shui promotes positive energy in the environment, the modern design industry has begun incorporating ideas from Feng Shui. Today, many developers, architects, and interior designers all over the world have started to include Feng Shui consultants on their project teams. Many students of the Feng Shui Interior Design online course that I teach are interior designers and architects, too.

I already introduced the basics of the Five Elements, including each of the directions (North, South, East, West, and their subparts), colors, shapes, and materials in chapter 1. In this chapter, I will add more details about each of these and also show how to use one of Feng Shui's most important tools—Bagua, or "Energy map." Here, we focus on the BTB-style Bagua, which contains eight ("Ba") areas ("Gua"), plus the center. These nine areas represent nine aspects of our life:

1. Family Gua: Wood (middle left)

2. Wealth & Prosperity Gua: Wood (rear left)

3. Fame & Reputation Gua: Fire (rear middle)

4. Love & Relationships Gua: Earth (rear right)

5. Children & Creativity Gua: Metal (middle right)

6. Travel & Helpful People Gua: Metal (front right)

7. Career Gua: Water (front middle)

8. Knowledge & Self-Cultivation Gua: Earth (front left)

9. Health Gua: Earth (center)

WEALTH + PROSPERITY	FAME + REPUTATION	RELATIONSHIPS
SE or Rear Left	S or R Middle	SW or Rear Right
Blue Wood Element	Red Fire Element	Pink Earth Element
FAMILY	**HEALTH**	**CHILDREN +**
E or Middle Left	(Middle)	**CREATIVITY**
Green Wood Element	Yellow, Earth Tones	W or Middle Right
		White Metal Element
KNOWLEDGE +	**CAREER**	**TRAVEL + HELPFUL**
SELF-CULTIVATION	N or	**PEOPLE**
NE or Front Left	Front Middle	NW or Front Right
Blue Earth Element	Black Water Element	Gray Metal Element

FIGURE 9. BTB- STYLE BAGUA

Bagua is a powerful tool that can help you reach your goals.

For Feng Shui beginners, I am presenting BTB Bagua in a simple way, since this book is an introduction and BTB is the most practiced form of Feng Shui in the Western world. If you're interested in learning more about the Compass School and its Bagua* as well, then this introductory book has accomplished one of its goals: to inspire you to learn more about the Feng Shui world!

HOW TO MAKE A BAGUA FLOOR PLAN

1. First, pull out your home's floor plan. If you don't have one, you can sketch it by hand.

2. Be sure to keep the front door of your house or apartment at the bottom of the floor plan.

3. Draw four evenly spaced lines horizontally and four vertically on the plan so that you form nine squares (as shown in Figure 10), reflecting the eight Gua (eight areas) plus the center (making nine areas in all).

4. Shade each Gua with its color, as shown in Figure 9.

5. Apply Feng Shui with your desired intention on each Gua. For example, if you seek luck in business, you may hang a piece of art depicting a water feature, such as a river or the ocean, on the wall, and a round mirror in the entrance hall in Career Gua. I provide recommendations for applying each Gua in Figure 10. Try it out and be creative. Enjoy!

---

*Bagua in Figure 9 contains actual compass directions used in the Compass School. The Compass School and the BTB School can sometimes differ in the recommendations they offer to resolve Feng Shui issues.

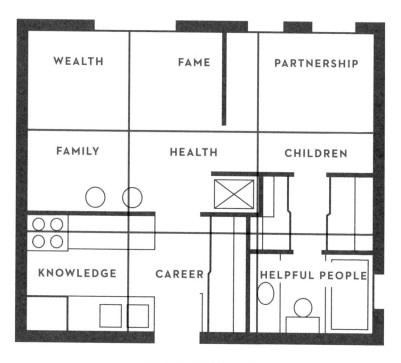

FIGURE 10. WAYS TO APPLY GUA

BTB's Bagua is always based on the front door location. Since the front door is always at the bottom, it can only fall in one of three Gua: Travel & Helpful People Gua (front right), Career Gua (front center), or Knowledge & Self-Cultivation Gua (front left).

This is the basic way in which you place Bagua on the whole house floor plan, which is called the Big Bagua. Later, you can also place Bagua on an individual room (Small Bagua). If you do, be sure to keep the entryway of the room on the bottom of the Bagua. You can even place Bagua on your desk. In that case, the side of the desk where you sit should be on the bottom.

FENG SHUI APPLICATION BY BAGUA

So far, you have learned the basics of Yin Yang Theory and the Five Elements, how energy flows, how to analyze a space, and how to treat problematic placements and enhance the energy in your home. Now you can apply more detailed Feng Shui principles by using Bagua. With the information here, you can also work on each room—including the entrance, the living room, the bedroom, the kitchen, and the bathroom. For now, become familiar with each Gua's meaning, the Five Elements, colors, shapes, materials, and useful items. You may find it fun to consider what could work in which area and how to implement those changes while looking at this Bagua information. Use what you already have, as well as your creativity and intuition.

Family Gua: Wood (middle left)

- **ACTUAL DIRECTION:** East (which is filled with the most auspicious Chi)
- **COLOR:** Green (since Water supports Wood, the Water element's colors—black and navy blue—are also good)
- **SHAPES:** Rectangular, tall, vertical
- **MATERIAL:** Wood
- **EXAMPLES:** Living plants and flowers, flower- and plant-printed or striped fabric, family photos, water fountains, mirrors, water-related items such as glass, photos or artwork depicting a river or a waterfall

This area may be good for a kid's room, since children's energy is growing like Wood energy. Rooms such as a living room or a dining room, where family and friends gather and enjoy spending time together, are a good fit for this Gua as well.

Wealth & Prosperity Gua: Wood (rear left)

- **ACTUAL DIRECTION:** Southeast
- **COLORS:** Purple, Green (since Water supports Wood, the Water element's color—black and navy blue—are also good)
- **SHAPES:** Rectangular, tall, vertical
- **MATERIAL:** Wood
- **EXAMPLES:** Living plants and flowers, flower-printed fabric, family photos, water fountains, mirrors, water-related items such as glass, photos or artwork depicting a river or a waterfall

Like Family Gua, this area may be good for a kid's room or a common area, such as a living room, a dining room, a kitchen. If you want to have luck in accumulating wealth, activate this area by adding plants and water features, some amethyst, or Chinese coins.

Fame & Reputation Gua: Fire (rear middle)

- **DIRECTION:** South
- **COLORS:** Red, orange (since Wood supports Fire, the Wood element's colors of green and purple are also good)
- **SHAPES:** Triangular, sharp
- **MATERIALS:** Fire, light, leather, fur
- **EXAMPLES:** Animal-printed cushions, a leather couch, candles, artwork depicting a horse or phoenix (a red bird), abstract art, trophies (since Fire is supported by Wood, Wood-related items are also good)

This area is good for a living room or an entrance hall. If you need recognition from the public (for example, if you're a celebrity) and want a good reputation, activate this area using Fire element features.

Love & Relationships Gua: Earth (rear right)

- **DIRECTION:** Southwest
- **COLORS:** Pink, yellow, brown (since Fire supports Earth, the Fire element's color—red—is also good)
- **SHAPES:** Rectangular, low, horizontal
- **MATERIALS:** Soil, pottery, brick
- **EXAMPLES:** Rose quartz, bright light, images of a matriarch or lovers

(since Earth is supported by Fire, Fire-related items are good as well)

This area is good for a master bedroom for a married couple, a kitchen, or a dining room. If you are looking for a good love life, a happy marriage, or fertility, activate this area by adding Earth and Fire element features.

Children & Creativity Gua: Metal (middle right)

- **DIRECTION:** West
- **COLORS:** White, gray (since Earth supports Metal, the Earth element's colors of pink, yellow, and brown are also good)
- **SHAPES:** Round, spherical
- **MATERIALS:** Metallic, particularly silver and gold
- **EXAMPLES:** A round gold clock, gold coins, a statue of elephants, a picture of pomegranates (since Metal is supported by Earth, Earth-related items are good, too)

This area is good for a bedroom, a recreation room, or a living room.

Travel & Helpful People Gua: Metal (front right)

- **DIRECTION:** Northwest
- **COLORS:** Gray, white (since Earth supports Metal, the Earth element's colors of pink, yellow, and brown are also good)
- **SHAPES:** Round, spherical
- **MATERIALS:** Metals, particularly silver and gold

- **EXAMPLES:** A round gold clock, coins (since Metal is supported by Earth, Earth-related items are also good)

This area is good for a bedroom, a study, a den, or a home office. When you need support from your boss, activate energy in this area.

Career Gua: Water (front middle)

- **DIRECTION:** North
- **COLORS:** Black, navy blue (since Metal supports Water, the Metal element's colors—gray and white—are also good)
- **SHAPES:** Wavy, curvy, irregular
- **MATERIALS:** Water, glass
- **EXAMPLES:** A fish tank, a small water fountain, flowers in a vase, a mirror, water-related artwork and photos (since Water is supported by Metal, Metal-related items are good, too)

If you are seeking greater success in your career, activate this area with Water element features.

Knowledge & Self Cultivation Gua: Earth (front left)

- **DIRECTION:** Northeast
- **COLORS**: Blue, yellow, brown (since Fire supports Earth, the Fire element's color of red is also good)
- **SHAPE:** Rectangular
- **MATERIALS:** Pottery, soil, brick
- **EXAMPLES:** Photos or artwork of mountains, crystal globes, sturdy

furniture (since Earth is supported by Fire, Fire-related items are good, too)

This is a good for a room for studying. If you are looking for success in your education or an examination for school or licensing, activate energy in this area by adding Earth element features.

Health Gua: Earth (center)

- **DIRECTION:** Center
- **COLORS:** Yellow, earthy colors (since Fire supports Earth, the Fire element's color of red is also good)
- **SHAPES:** Rectangular, low, horizontal
- **MATERIALS:** Pottery, soil, brick
- **EXAMPLES:** Low-slung furniture, a ceramic vase, pottery (since Earth is supported by Fire, Fire-related items also work)

The center area in any space or building is considered to be a very important spot, so you should always keep this area clean.

A FEW WORDS OF CAUTION

There is a reason I keep emphasizing that you should take time applying Feng Shui principles.

Bagua is a really powerful tool that is based on the ancient Chinese *I Ching* (*The Book of Changes*). It does change the energy in your house, if you work with a very clear, focused, and positive mindset. Are you ready for a change? Are you sure you can receive a new opportunity when it comes your way? I warn you: If you change the energy in the space too quickly, sometimes (especially if you are a sensitive person) your body and mind will not keep up with the speed of the changing energy in the space. This may cause you to experience some physical or emotional reactions, such as fatigue, headache, or anxiety. Imagine if the energy of your space had been negative, stagnant, and stuck for long time, and suddenly you clear up the space and apply Feng Shui quickly. The energy will start flowing quickly, as if you had suddenly released stagnant water from a dam. Some people may feel the change physically or emotionally—others may not feel anything at all. This is why I emphasize that this process takes a fair amount of time.

You have to maintain a very clear and positive intention during this process—this is one of the reasons BTB Feng Shui suggests meditation as an adjunct to the Feng Shui process. When you apply Feng Shui to your space, you are calling for the Universe to manifest your desires, dreams, and goals. When the change—whether small or big—comes, do not forget to thank the Universe for giving you this opportunity. You may get a promotion at work, even though you wanted to manifest a love relationship. Change may come in a fashion that you did not expect, or it may come at an unexpected time. Even so, I want you to be open to and appreciative of any changes that come to you while you're engaging in Feng Shui. Sometimes change may seem undesirable at first, but with the passage of time, when you see the whole picture, that change may have had to happen to allow you to reach your ultimate goal. When you are truly connected and harmonized with yourself, the people around you, the energy in the environment, the cycle of nature, and universal energy, you are mentally, physically, and spiritually balanced and at peace. This is the best condition to be in, because you'll be able to receive and accept the positive changes that you seek.

Also, when you use Bagua for your home in practicing Feng Shui, be mindful that you don't need to use all the colors and items that Bagua suggests. There are no strict rules that you must follow. Use Bagua as a guideline. You should also trust your gut feelings and intuitions. There may be other aspects that you may also need to consider: your preferences (and those of your family or partner, if you live with them), functionality, and the design-style balance, among others.

Start little by little, doing things that make sense to you. I've seen people who think Feng Shui is too complicated for them to practice because of the many rules—something I totally understand. But I know, as a consultant, that it is not possible for us to follow all the Feng Shui rules perfectly. Sometimes you will not like some Feng Shui suggestions that come from Bagua; that's understandable. Do not worry that, if you don't follow the suggestions, bad luck will come. It will not. Be open, flexible, creative, and playful with whatever you think you could apply. Again, remember that Feng Shui can be Fun Shui! This especially applies to BTB's

Feng Shui, as it is very simple to apply, so I believe you will find it enjoyable to practice in your home.

In the next chapter, we will learn how to apply simple Feng Shui room by room: entrance, living room, bedroom, kitchen, and bathroom. Are you ready?

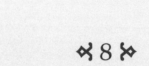

HOW TO APPLY FENG SHUI TO YOUR SPACE, ROOM BY ROOM

I N THIS CHAPTER, I WOULD LIKE TO INTRODUCE SIMPLE FENG SHUI
applications room by room: entrance, living room, bedroom,
kitchen, and bathroom. These principles can be used in your
home, your office, or anywhere else. You can work on each room with
the five simple steps I introduce here, as well as using the Bagua floor
plan that you learned to make in the previous chapter.

When you apply Feng Shui to your home, the very first thing you
need to understand is that each room of your house has its own purpose
and personality. Think about whether each room is serving its purpose—are you letting the room play its proper role? For example, if you
use your entry hall for storage and place random things there, you may
be preventing it from fulfilling its intended role.

One thing I want to emphasize is that, as I noted previously, please
do not feel overwhelmed or think that you have to follow all these rules
strictly. Feng Shui may seem to have so many rules, and some Feng
Shui suggestions sometimes may not relate to you at all. It's normal to

be a bit intimidated. Even I do not follow all the Feng Shui rules, because that is impossible. So my suggestion for you is to start with something that makes sense to you first and see how you feel. If you like it and it feels good, then add the next one. Remember to always pay attention to the balance of Yin Yang and the Five Elements in the space. When you achieve a good balance of Yin and Yang with an appropriate application of Five Elements items in harmonized furniture layouts, you may find that the other Feng Shui rules fall into place. (You may want to review the information on this in chapters 5 and 6.)

So, try to implement these five simple steps, room by room, at your own pace without any stress. Enjoy the process. Some of you may want to get everything done right away to see the results, but, unfortunately, that is not how this works. Working on your home is the same process as working on yourself—you have to do it gradually. But believe me, you will find it fun if you proceed at your own pace!

STEP 1: THE ENTRANCE

First, let's check the entrance area of your home.

The entrance is the first place you step into when you come home from outside. It is the connector between the outside world and your home. In Feng Shui, the entrance area is considered to be one of the most important areas, along with the bedroom and the kitchen, because the main entry door is a "Mouth of Chi," where energy comes into the house from outside. This means that the entrance area's purpose is to welcome good energy as well as to welcome you, your family, and your guests. Therefore, this area should be neither cluttered nor dirty. I always suggest that my clients work on this area first, and once they finish this step, they always tell me, "Ai, I can feel the energy already starting to change!" I hope you will, too.

1. Space Clearing

Get rid of garbage or junk, piles of old newspapers and mail, and cardboard, and dust to clear the space. If there are many pairs of shoes on the floor, they should be placed in a shoe rack. A vacuum cleaner or trash bin is not supposed to be here—put them somewhere else, such as in a closet, because they are not welcoming. The entrance or hallway is not a storage area. I know that this may sound obvious, but, believe me, this is a common issue.

If the doormat is old and worn out, replace it with a new one. If you do not have one, get one. Doormats absorb negative energy that we carry from the outside, and they can filter negative energy when we step on them.

2. Check the Placement / Layout

Be mindful of the location of a mirror in the entryway. Hanging a mirror on the wall facing toward the main front door is considered bad Feng Shui, since it pushes good energy trying to come in back out. If you have some other problems with your layout, try to remedy them as best you can. (Refer to chapter 6.)

3. Check the Yin Yang Balance

The entrance should have Yang energy. Good energy does not want to come into a dark entrance, so try to keep it bright by keeping the light on if there's not much sunlight. I suggest hanging a crystal chandelier or a crystal ball from the ceiling if the entryway is aligned with another door or a window, because the good energy can run through and out of your home quickly if it is not interrupted. (Refer to ways to use crystal balls in chapter 6.)

4. Check the Five Elements Cycle

If the entrance area is too plain, you may want to place some nice decorations and living plants or a flower arrangement there to add more warm, welcoming vibes. If it is difficult to do so, you could consider hanging artwork or photos depicting nature, based on Bagua, instead. A wind chime by the door will provide beautiful sounds, and flowers are helpful both for their visual appeal as well as their aroma—they also create good Feng Shui and welcome good energy.

If your entrance area falls in the Travel & Helpful People Gua, or the Northwest side of the house (see page 73), you may consider adding some Metal items to activate these Gua, particularly if you seek luck with travel and supporters. For example, a framed photo of the place where you want to travel, a metal wind chime affixed to the door, or a gold- or silver-framed round mirror would do nicely. You may also add some Earth element items, since Earth is a supporter for Metal. (Refer to the Five Element Cycle in chapter 2.)

Do not focus too much on Metal only. Blend it with other elements in harmony.

Try to utilize Bagua (see chapter 7), and apply colors, materials, items, and art based on it. Of course, do not forget to use your own creativity, too!

When I visit a client's house for a Feng Shui consultation, the first thing I check is the entry area. I do so because this is the place where you welcome yourself, your people, and good energy. It is not far-fetched to say that how you welcome yourself to your home parallels how you welcome good luck and energy into your home. Imagine that you are on vacation, entering a hotel. Would you feel more welcomed by a spacious, bright space with a beautiful flower arrangement, nice scents, and the smiles of the hotel receptionist? Or a by small, dark entrance area with a weird scent and unsmiling staff? Obviously, the first one, right? It is not necessary to decorate your home's entrance to make it look like a luxury hotel, but the key is to show your effort to make the space better and manifest your intentions to the Universe. That way, the Universe will recognize your message and provide what you seek. Be better, do better, and receive good fortune.

Here is an interesting example. I once had a client who never used her entrance door. Instead, she used the back door because it was convenient for her. I advised her to start using the front door, because how she enters the house could confuse the Universe. The

Universe is willing to send us good energy, which usually enters from the main door of the house, not the back door. Her habit could be misunderstood by the Universe to believe that in that home, there is nobody welcoming good energy. If so, the good energy will go somewhere else. Since she never used the front door, the entryway was cluttered with random things, which showed the Universe that she was not ready to welcome good luck. To make matters worse, the back door where she entered her home led to the kitchen, and the first thing she would see when entering was a garbage can. Obviously, good luck can and will refuse to enter the house that way. After the consultation, she took my advice and, later (actually a few hours later!), she received a phone call from someone she really loved from her past. One of the reasons she had a Feng Shui consultation with me was that she wanted to enhance her love energy and meet the right person. You may think that call was a coincidence or a miracle, but to a Feng Shui consultant, this is normal, because that is how the Universe functions. This is how its energy works, and Feng Shui is how you can make it work for you.

STEP 2: THE LIVING ROOM

Now, let's check the living room. The living room is a place where you, your family, and your guests will enjoy time together, feeling entertained or relaxed. Is your living room conducive to entertaining and relaxing? To work on the living room, check the following points:

1. Space Clearing

Clean and declutter as much as you can. Get rid of or relocate any items that do not fit there. Do not store things in your living room.

2. Check Placement / Layout

Does the energy flow smoothly in the space? Is anything blocking the door or a window? Is the furniture placed in a stable fashion that makes you feel secure? Large furniture in a living room, such as a sofa, TV set, or bookshelf should be placed against a solid wall for support. It is ideal to locate your sofa in a command position, facing the entry, if possible. If it is difficult to do so because of the room structure, you can consider using a mirror to allow you to see the entry of the living room in its reflection. If you have some other problematic layout, try to treat as much as you can. As we have discussed, there are many options (refer to chapter 6).

3. Check the Yin Yang Balance

The living room is the most Yang place in the house. It's where you and your friends or family will enjoy conversation, watching movies, listening to music, and having fun together. Yang products—such as a TV, stereo, musical instruments, and books are appropriate here. Beautiful artwork, plants, and lighting are also important to create Yang energy. If you prefer to have more low-key, relaxing vibes, reduce the Yang portion a bit and add a few Yin features. This might mean toning down the color scheme with earthy or monotone colors and adding some furniture that has a round or curvy shape. Make sure you have a good lighting system and window treatments, so that you can adjust sunlight, depending on the mood (excitement, relaxation) that you want to create.

4. Check the Five Element Balance

See if the colors, shapes, materials, and other item choices are well balanced. Make sure you do not use only one element in the space. For example, do not put all the Fire element features in the living room just because your living room is located in Fame & Reputation Gua, or the South side of the house. All Fire elements might look something like this: Leather sofa, red coffee table on an animal-print rug, many candles, bright lamps, and a lot of colorful framed art on the wall. The room will become too Yang, which may excite you too much and make you uncomfortable over time. Make sure to blend all the Five Elements wisely, based on your Bagua.

5. Other Matters

The living room is a good place to express your personality and share it with your family and guests. Anything related to your hobbies, interests, pictures of your family, awards that you received, and so forth can be displayed and shared here. If you need a home office to work remotely and you do not have an extra room for it, making one in the living room may be a good option.

STEP 3: THE BEDROOM

Now, take a look at the bedroom. The bedroom is a place where we rest and recharge our energy. Do you sleep well in your bedroom? In Feng Shui, the bedroom is considered one of the most important places in the home. Ideally, we spend almost eight hours—one-third of our day—in the bedroom, which means that the bedroom's condition can have a powerful effect on our energy. Review your bedroom to see if it serves its purpose for you. To work on the bedroom, take the following steps.

1. Space Clearing

Get rid of any non-bedroom items and relocate them where they belong. Are there piled-up clothes? They should be in the closet or dresser. Your vacuum cleaner should be in a closet. Do not store items under the bed, as that will interrupt energy flow.

2. Check Placement / Layout

See if the layout and placement are appropriate for smooth energy flow. If you have any problematic placements or layout, address them as much as you can. The ideal bed placement, as we discussed, is in the command position (see chapter 6). The headboard should abut a solid wall for support, and you should try to keep an equal space on both sides of the bed so that energy can flow in a balanced way. If this is difficult to do, because of limited space, even a few inches of space away from the wall on one side is better than nothing.

Do not place a mirror where you can see your reflection from the bed. This can disturb your sleep quality by reflecting your energy (see chapter 6).

Photos of your family or friends are unfavorable in the bedroom (better to have them in a common area, such as a living room or a dining room), especially if you are single and looking for love. Instead, display a photo or artwork of happy couples or pairs of birds, which manifest your love luck. If you are a married couple or in a relationship, it is okay to have pictures of the two of you together in the bedroom; in fact, this will enhance your love energy.

3. Check the Yin Yang Balance

The bedroom is a Yin place where you and your partner relax, sleep, and recharge. Yang products—electronic items, such as TV, audio devices, cell phones, and musical instruments—should not be here. If you wish to keep a TV in the bedroom, a Feng Shui consultant will not force you to remove it against your will, but may suggest that you cover the TV screen with a cloth when you're not watching it.

Make sure you have good lighting and window treatments that will allow you to maintain nicely balanced Yin vibes. Shut the curtains and the door when you go to sleep. You may want to use a lamp with a dimmer and leave it on at night to avoid complete darkness when you sleep, as too much Yin should be avoided. Additionally, it is ideal to have a pair of lamps on nightstands, one on each side of the bed (see chapter 6). However, neither side of the bed can abut the wall.

Plants are Wood elements, which bring uplifting Yang energy. Limited numbers of plants are fine to have in the bedroom, but if you have many plants there, that may interfere with the quality of your sleep, because sleeping is considered a Yin activity. You should avoid bringing too much Yang energy to the place that you sleep.

4. Check the Five Elements Balance

Cleanliness and tidiness are needed in the bedroom to maintain positive energy. Keep it as simple as possible with soothing decorations, based on Bagua: a bed, night tables, lamps, a clock, a rug, some nice art, and selected personal items are pretty much all you need. Avoid too many vivid colors, which would lead to too much Yang. For example, if your bedroom falls in the Knowledge & Self-Cultivation Gua, or the Northeast side of the home, you may hang on the wall a framed photo or piece of art depicting beautiful mountains, or a portrait of a historical person whose wisdom inspires you (for example, George Washington or Mother Teresa).

5. Other Matters

The bedroom is a very private place, where you connect with yourself and recharge your energy. It is not ideal to have a home office in the bedroom because sleeping is a Yin activity while working is a Yang activity.

But because of limited space, if your bedroom is the only option where you can have a home office, try to divide these two areas with a room divider or curtains so that at least you do not see your PC or other work-related items when you're in bed.

Most of my clients who have sleep issues have seen a positive result after they implement these suggested steps. If you have a health issue, poor quality of sleep may be one of the reasons. Implementing Feng Shui in your bedroom may improve your health and eventually make your energy more positive.

STEP 4: THE KITCHEN

The kitchen is a place to cook healthy food to feed yourself and your family. It relates to our health and our ability to make money. Therefore, the kitchen is considered to be an important area in Feng Shui because it affects the residents' financial luck.

The kitchen can be a tricky and chaotic place sometimes, though, both physically and energetically. Many things are going on there: stove, oven, microwave (Fire elements), a refrigerator and the sink (Water element), and then a bunch of different foods (wet or dry) and drinks. In this one space, a great deal of electrical energy is being consumed, too. Assess your kitchen using these guidelines.

1. Space Clearing

Clean and declutter as much as you can, because the kitchen tends to get dirty and cluttered with crumbs, dirty dishes, garbage, expired food, and oil. Get rid of all expired food from the refrigerator and pantry.

2. Check Placement / Layout

See if the layout and furniture placement are appropriate for smooth energy flow. If you have any problematic placements or layouts, address them as much as you can, especially if the kitchen entry is aligned with the main front door of the house (refer to chapter 6).

If the sink and the stove are aligned or next each other, an energy conflict may occur. To treat the energy conflict, you can place a potted plant between them if there's enough space for it. If not, you may hang crystal balls from the ceiling (refer to chapter 6).

If the stove and the kitchen entry are aligned so that you can't see the entrance while you're cooking, place a mirror near the stove so that you can see who's entering the kitchen.

3. Check the Yin Yang Balance

A kitchen is a Yang place, as cooking itself is a Yang activity and there are many Fire elements present. Maintain the uplifting Yang vibes here with good lighting and a few cool or earth-colored items, while being careful not to bring in too many more Fire (Yang) element features.

4. Check the Five Elements Balance

See if colors, shapes, materials, and other item choices are well balanced. Make sure you do not use only one element in the space. Try not to add too many Fire elements, such as red-colored items, candles, sharp-cornered furniture, bold design, fur, and leather products, because the kitchen already has a lot of Fire energy. Instead, add some natural, earthy color schemes, such as cream yellow or a nice soothing green, and potted plants in ceramic pots (Wood & Earth elements) to balance the energy.

Feng Shui suggests that the table in an eat-in kitchen be round or oval, rather than square or rectangular. This promotes a smoother flow of Chi at the table and makes your guests feel more comfortable at the table.

5. Other Matters

If your kitchen is in the center of your home, be extra careful about the cleanliness of the kitchen. In Feng Shui, it is not favorable to have the kitchen in the center of the house because it may cause health or wealth issues. The center of the house is considered to be "the heart" of the house, and the kitchen's Fire energy could burn it. Don't worry too much if your kitchen is in the center of the house, however; if so, obviously you are stuck with it. To address such a circumstance, I suggest that you do a careful Feng Shui analysis to ensure balance from a Yin Yang / Five Elements perspective, and to tame the kitchen's Fire energy.

STEP 5: THE BATHROOM

Finally, let's check the bathroom. The bathroom is a place where we clean our bodies every day. A bathroom is considered to be the most Yin place in the house, because it has so much Water energy. This area is often undermaintained, being the dirtiest place in the house, while other rooms like the living room or the kitchen are kept clean. No more—we should pay extra attention to the bathroom, because an excess of Water energy, especially if it's dirty, can drain good energy and affect our health and wealth as a result.

Check the following points and make sure you take care of the bathroom appropriately to protect your health and wealth luck.

1. Space Clearing

Make sure the bathroom is always clean and tidy. Try to keep loose items in a medicine cabinet, on a shelf, or on shower rack so that there is nothing on the surface of the sink.

2. Check Placement / Layout

See if the layout and placement are appropriate for smooth energy flow. If you have any problematic placements or layout, address them as much as you can, especially if the bathroom door is aligned with the main front door of the house (see chapter 6).

If the toilet and the bathroom door are aligned, good energy can be quickly drained. To prevent this, you may hang a crystal ball from the ceiling between the toilet and the door (see chapter 6). Most importantly, make sure to always close the toilet lid and keep the bathroom door shut.

3. Check the Yin Yang Balance

Since the bathroom is the most Yin place in the house, it may easily become dirty, dark, and wet. Be sure keep the space clean, bright, and dry. To bring in Yang energy, keep a low-wattage bathroom light on as much as you can. (Some Feng Shui consultants suggest leaving the bathroom light on all the time.)

If the bathroom has a window, open it when the weather permits for air circulation and to prevent mold. If your bathroom does not have a window, keep the fan on for a certain period of time every day to prevent humidity from forming.

Avoid use of a dark color scheme (black, charcoal gray, dark blue) in the bathroom because that enhances Yin energy. White is always good, since it provides a clean image in the space.

4. Check the Five Elements Balance

Cleanliness, brightness, and circulation are more important than decoration in the bathroom. Keep your decor as simple and soothing as possible, based on Bagua. To tame the prevalent Water energy, a plant in a ceramic pot is suggested. The Wood element can exhaust the Water element, according to the Five Element cycle. This is called the Depleting Cycle, which is in between the Productive Cycle and the Controlling Cycle that I discussed in chapter 2.

5. Other Issues

In addition to placing potted plants in the bathroom, if the humidity there tends to be high, you may try adding Earth element features (for more information on the Controlling Cycle, see chapter 2).

Your house may have more rooms, such as a dining room, a den, etc., but you can take the same steps for them.

MORE PERSONALIZED FENG SHUI?

If you want to add much more detailed Feng Shui, you may want to try Mingua (refer to the appendix), which can tell you your personal Five Elements, by checking your Kua Number based on your birth year (see the appendix). Mingua is a part of the Compass School's techniques; therefore, I won't discuss them too deeply in this book. However, it is very helpful to know your Kua Number, which can provide insight into your personal traits, as well as the compatibility between you, your family, and your friends. This allows you to be in harmony not only with the environment but also in relationships, which I will discuss in the next chapter.

HOW TO APPLY FENG SHUI TO YOUR RELATIONSHIP

YOU MAY BE SURPRISED TO LEARN THAT WE CAN APPLY FENG Shui to relationships. Yes, we can. Remember Yin Yang Theory and the Five Elements cycle that you learned about in chapter 2? We will use that system to identify people's personality traits and assess the compatibility between you and the people in your life.

First, we will learn the Yin type of personality and the Yang type of personality. Later, I will introduce you to eight different types of personality, based on the Five Elements, using Kua Number (see appendix). These personality types are not necessarily good or bad; rather, we are just identifying the characteristics the person has, because all of us have both Yin and Yang sides to us and some or all of the Five Elements aspects.

A YIN PERSONALITY MAY BE:

- Feminine
- Passive
- Indirect
- Good at listening
- Soft-spoken
- Inexpressive
- Slow to make a decision
- Logical rather than emotional
- Favoring smaller groups
- Preferring stability rather than adventure
- Private
- Good at planning, as opposed to executing
- Compassionate

A YANG PERSONALITY MAY BE:

- Masculine
- Active
- Direct
- Good at speaking
- Convincing as a speaker
- Expressive
- Quick at making decisions
- Emotional rather than logical
- Loud
- Favoring socializing in a bigger group

- Preferring to take risks, rather than settling for the status quo
- Open
- Preferring to take action, rather than planning
- Competitive

We all have qualities of both Yin and Yang. Depending on the situation, or the roles you play in society or at work, you may need to play up your Yin or your Yang sometimes. For example, by nature, you may be a Yin person—inexpressive, passive, soft-spoken—but at work, as a leader managing many employees, the Yang side of your personality might need to come to the fore, as you must quickly make decisions and speak convincingly and passionately to motivate your team.

FIVE ELEMENTS PERSONALITY TRAITS BY KUA NUMBER

You can identify Five Elements characteristic traits by checking your Kua Number (see appendix), and seeing which group (the East Group or the West Group) you belong to. Whoever is in the same group as you will have good compatibility with you; conversely, whoever is in the other group may be difficult in a relationship with you. After you check yours, check your family and friends' groups.

The East Group: Kua Numbers 1, 3, 4, and 9

The best four directions for the East Group are South, Southeast, East, and North. Try to arrange your bed so that your head points in one of these directions. Also, try to arrange your desk so that you face one of these directions while seated.

KUA NUMBER 1 (ELEMENT: WATER)

- Creative
- Flexible
- Independent
- Business-minded
- Mysterious
- Self-indulgent

BEST COLORS: Black, dark blue

BEST DIRECTIONS: Southeast, East, South, North

KUA NUMBER 3 (ELEMENT: WOOD/THUNDER)

- Goal-oriented
- Works well under pressure
- A good leader
- Intelligent
- Stubborn
- Inflexible

BEST COLORS: Green, blue, black

BEST DIRECTIONS: South, Southeast, East

KUA NUMBER 4 (ELEMENT: WOOD/WIND)

- Sociable

- Organized
- Loyal
- Loves learning new things
- Indecisive
- Arrogant

BEST COLORS: Green, blue, black

BEST DIRECTIONS: North, South, East, Southeast

KUA NUMBER 9 (ELEMENT: FIRE)

- Charismatic
- Energetic
- Enthusiastic
- Competitive
- Argumentative
- Overindulgent

BEST COLORS: Red, Purple, Pink, Green

BEST DIRECTIONS: East, Southeast, North, South

THE WEST GROUP: KUA NUMBERS 2, 5, 6, 7, AND 8

The best four directions for the West Group are West, Northwest, Southwest, and Northeast. Again, try to arrange your bed so that your head points toward one of these directions. Similarly, try to arrange your desk so that you face one of these directions while you are seated.

Kua Number 2 (Element: Earth)

- Stable
- Reliable
- A good caregiver
- Patient
- Takes on too much responsibility
- Insecure

BEST COLORS: Beige, yellow, orange

BEST FOUR DIRECTIONS: Northeast, West, Northwest, Southwest

Kua Number 5 (Center)

Kua Number 5 is divided into male and female, since it represents the combination of Yin and Yang Chi energies.

- Males will use the Kua Number 2, above.
- Females will use the Kua Number 8, below.

Kua Number 6 (Element: Metal/Heaven)

- Dignified
- Knowledgeable
- Analytical
- A good leader
- Inflexible
- Judgmental

BEST COLORS: White, gray, gold, silver, yellow

BEST FOUR DIRECTIONS: West, Northeast, Southwest, Northwest

Kua Number 7 (Element: Metal / Lake)

- Optimistic
- Artistic
- Graceful
- Creative
- Critical
- Picky

BEST COLORS: White, gray, gold, silver, yellow

BEST FOUR DIRECTIONS: Northwest, Southwest, Northeast, West

Kua Number 8 (Element: Earth / Mountain)

- Focused
- Persistent
- A great problem solver
- Goal-oriented
- Stubborn
- Resistant to change

BEST COLORS: Blue, yellow, orange, beige

BEST FOUR DIRECTIONS: Southwest, Northwest, West, Northeast

RELATIONSHIP IN THE PRODUCTIVE CYCLE

According to Five Elements cycle diagram (see page 22), Water supports Wood, Wood supports Fire, Fire supports Earth, Earth supports Metal, Metal supports Water. When you are with someone who has a supporter element, you may feel secure, encouraged, and motivated in the relationship.

For example, if your Kua Number is 9 and your partner's is 3, this means your Five Element is Fire and theirs is Wood/Thunder. Their Wood energy (goal-oriented, idealistic) and personality traits fuel your Fire energy and personality traits, just as Wood supports Fire. For example, if the other person is your boss, their vision, plans, and goals inspire you, motivate you, and fuel you to execute those plans and work hard to make the project successful. When people are in such a cycle, they are generally happy with each other and very compatible over the long term.

RELATIONSHIP IN THE CONTROLLING CYCLE

On the other hand, when a relationship is in the Controlling Cycle, things can be challenging. According to the Five Elements cycle diagram (see page 22), Water is a controller for Fire, Fire for Metal, Metal for Wood, Wood for Earth, Earth for Water. When you are with someone who has a controlling element, you may feel pressured, overpowered, and insecure.

For example, if your Kua Number is 2 and your partner's is 1, your Five Element is Earth and theirs is Water. Your Earth energy and personality traits (stability, security, reliability) may overpower their Water energy and personality traits (flexible, creative, vague), much in the way that Earth (soil) dams Water. For example, if the person is your partner, their thinking and communication style may appear too vague and structureless in your eyes. This may make you feel frustrated because you seek a secure and solid relationship (for example, engagement, marriage, or some other sort of commitment), but your partner prefers to keep things more amorphous. (In your personal dictionary, there is no such phrase as "Go with the flow.") With their creative, free-flowing mindset, they may feel pressured by your energy. For example, if you are an Earth mother with a Water son, take a moment to make sure that you are not interfering too much with his unique, creative, and free nature with your high expectations, based on the common sense.

When people are in this cycle, each of them must make an effort to keep the relationship healthy and respectful by learning how to communicate with each other.

Even if you do not know a person's Kua Number, you may see what type of Five Element quality, or at least Yin Yang qualities, they may have by observing their behavior, tone of voice, fashion sense, and how they carry themselves. If you see someone who is direct, outspoken, enthusiastic, high energy, very competitive, emotional, expressive, and inspiring, they have Fire element personality traits. On the other hand, if someone is more logical, knowledgeable, critical, a careful thinker, detail-oriented, a perfectionist, inexpressive, and data-oriented, they have Metal element personality traits.

In Feng Shui, relationships in the Controlling Cycle are considered challenging. I've seen many couples in this cycle experience a hard time in their relationship. Feng Shui, however, does not suggest that they should divorce or break up. On the contrary, they may make a great team whose traits complement each other if they respect their differences in values. To reach that level, each of them must put in a great deal of effort to learn each other's language, which will allow them to better communicate. One of my clients (Fire—emotional, active, passionate, influential) had been suffering in her relationship with her husband (Water—creative, flexible, not set in stone, vague). When I visited her house for the first time, I did not see anything that reflected her personality, only his. The home revealed that she was suppressing her energy. The interior color scheme was mostly dark (Water), which brought more Yin vibes to the space. Further, the furniture placement did not promote open communication, so we implemented some Feng Shui adjustments to better allow her Fire energy to express itself; this, in turn, enabled her to better express herself. We promoted harmony by adding more warm colors, relocated the furniture for better energy flow, brought in more plants (Wood) to boost her Fire energy, while taming her husband's Water energy, and injected other Five Elements to allow better circulation in the space.

In the process, she learned how much she had not been expressing her true thoughts and feelings to her husband, because she had been afraid to bother him. She also learned that her fear stemmed from her insecurity and low self-esteem, which had formed through the dynamics from her family of origin, dating back to childhood.

Through the process of working on her Feng Shui home project, she gradually started to understand the dynamics of her relationship with her husband and how to share her emotional needs and opinions with him. Her husband was open to supporting and encouraging her. By the time the home project was complete, she had gained more self-esteem and confidence, accomplished a life goal, and started living in a more positive way. These qualities all enhanced the quality of her relationship with her husband.

All relationships have ups and downs, but a strong, healthy relationship with other people can be established only when we have self-acceptance and self-love. Without being connected with ourselves, it is impossible to be connected with other people in true harmony.

What Feng Shui can teach us in terms of relationships is actually the same as what we can learn about the environment through its use: Promote smooth energy flow to be in harmony. In order to Feng Shui our relationship with the people in our lives, first we must know ourselves, then use that information to assess our relationships with others. Through this process, we can identify the dynamics of a relationship, figure out how to complement each other by respecting each other's different personality traits and talents, and work toward living in harmony.

✧ 10 ✧

FENG SHUI LIFESTYLE

Now you've been introduced to the basics of Feng Shui, including its theories, history, styles, techniques, and applications. Feng Shui is a lifestyle; it is a way to live in harmony, and it is totally up to you how you choose to implement it. If this book inspires you to choose to live in harmony with your own being, with people around you, with your surrounding environment, with the cycles of nature, and with the universal order, that is the beginning of living the Feng Shui lifestyle.

Remember the Yin Yang symbol that I showed you on page 20? That simple symbol from Taoism shows us everything there is know about being in harmony. The idea of the Yin Yang symbol suggests that everything exists in duality, which is the law of nature and the Universe. Feng Shui teaches us to live with the flow of nature's pattern. The world changes constantly, and moves forward with cycles, just like the Yin Yang symbol: The day turns into night and the night turns into the next morning and goes on. Everything that is born and lives eventually dies and another new being is born. Likewise, the concept of "right" cannot exist without the corresponding concept of "wrong." "Positive" and "negative," "good luck" and "bad luck," "happy" and "sad" and all the other opposing elements are interdependent and cannot exist without the other. We can feel happiness because we know sadness, and appreciation of happiness gives us more strength to weather sadness in the future. Today may be a good day; we hope tomorrow will be the same. But sometimes we have a bad day as well. The bad days help us to grow and improve, and we live with the knowledge that there will be another good day in the future. That is the way of nature. We will always have good days and bad days, sunny days and rainy days, successful days and stressful days. Feng Shui is a way to live with "Tao" (the Way) and Taoism, not to go against the Way. Feng Shui is neither a religion nor a science, but a way for us to live in harmony with others and the Universe.

As I discussed in chapter 3, "History of Feng Shui," Feng Shui is part of Traditional Chinese Medicine and shares its theories with acupuncture. I myself am not an acupuncturist, but, before I started my Feng Shui consulting business, I worked for one of the largest US-based Asian medical colleges; these teach Traditional Chinese Medicine. (Back then, I did not even expect I would ever be a professional Feng Shui consultant, but looking back to those days, I realize that I was in pretty deep in the Feng Shui world!) As a member of the school staff, I utilized one of the employee benefits—free weekly acupuncture treatments after work, which was done by interns, each with a supervisor. Before the actual treatment, the intern and supervisor always asked me detailed questions about my lifestyle: my sleeping patterns, my menstrual cycle, my eating habits, my drinking habits, exercise, stress, physical pain, my emotional state. They would ask me multiple questions. For instance, they asked questions about my sleeping habits, such as: Do you sleep well? When did you go to sleep last night, and what time did you wake up this morning? Do you wake up before morning, and, if so, how many times, and what time did that happen? Do you sweat while you're sleeping? Do you grind your teeth? Do you remember your dreams? How do you feel after you dream? At first, I found it a bit hard to answer all the questions clearly because I did not remember so many things about how I lived my daily life, but due to these weekly acupuncture treatments, I started paying more attention to my health. The interns kept records on patient cards and every time I visited, they updated my card, based on my answers that day. They checked my weight, pulse, temperature, and blood pressure, and they examined my tongue ("tongue diagnosis" is very important in Traditional Chinese Medicine). As I lay on the bed waiting for the intern and the supervisor, sometimes I heard them discussing which acupoints they should approach, and one day an intern explained to me, "I will needle this X point to stimulate the kidney, which is a Water element, and it will enhance your liver, a Wood element." I was very excited, because that's how Feng Shui works in a physical space as well!

I enjoyed these weekly acupuncture treatments, and, in the end, the advice was always the same, which was pretty simple: Go to bed by 11 p.m.; sleep eight hours; eat a healthy, balanced diet; drink lots of water; refrain from drinking too much alcohol; exercise; breathe well (that is, meditate); and keep your body warm to promote better blood flow.

Without adopting this simple basic lifestyle, living in the harmony that Taoism teaches us cannot happen. Going to bed by 11 p.m., or at the latest by 1 a.m., is crucial to maintaining healthy Yin Yang / Five Element energy in our bodies. Morning (Wood) to noon (Fire), when the sun is high in the sky, is Yang time, and our body cycle works naturally following the day's cycle, too. Morning sunlight has positive Yang energy, which you should not waste by sleeping in just because you were watching YouTube videos until late at night. Open the window when you get up in the morning, breathe in the fresh morning air, and let the morning Yang energy flow into your body and into your home. When the sun reaches the highest point in the sky, at noon, that is the most Yang time of the day. Therefore, to be in harmony with your body and follow the cycle of nature, it is highly recommended to do all active and creative work (your daily work, exercise, or study) during Yang time, because that is the time when your body and brain perform the best.

From late afternoon/early evening (Earth) toward evening/night (Metal), the day gradually shifts to Yin time, while our body does as well. This is a time to enjoy dinner with family, partners, or friends;

spend some quality time with them, sharing what happened during the day; or read books, watch movies, have a nice hot bath, stretch, meditate, and go to sleep. Midnight (Water) is the most Yin time of the day, and sleeping is the most Yin activity in our daily life. Without having good Yin (rest), your body and mind won't be ready to perform well (Yang) the next morning (Wood, again). (We can see the pattern of the Yin Yang / Five Elements cycle not only in a twenty-four-hour day, but also in the twelve months of the year.) This is why sleep quality is crucial and why making a good Feng Shui bedroom arrangement is very important for us. If your bedroom has too much Yang (too bright, too many windows with outside views, a mirror facing toward you in bed, a lot of electronic devices, doing web surfing on your smartphone in bed until late), of course, your sleep quality becomes poor. That's because your environment, body, and mindset are too Yang, which goes against the natural cycle.

When we have an unbalanced Yin Yang / Five Elements energy cycle in our lifestyle for a long time, our body clock gets stuck in an irregular cycle, which goes against the course of nature. As a result, we may have physical or mental issues that may manifest as fatigue, hair loss, poor sleep, constipation, weight gain, a weak immune system, an irregular menstrual cycle, extreme premenstrual syndrome, anxiety, depression, or anger. When I have a health problem, I ascribe it to some unbalanced energy in my life. Paying attention to small changes in our health condition, emotional state, surrounding environment, and relationships can help us to live in harmony.

That said, being in harmony does not mean that we always have to be "positive" and deny our "negative" side. No. As I said previously, Yin and Yang comprise a set of two opposing energies—they do not suggest that we should exist on only one side. It is like a coin with a front and a reverse side. We should see things in dual dimensions. When a good thing happens, that appears to be positive. But like the flip side of a coin, there is always a possibility that a bad thing could happen as well, which may appear to be negative. This Yin Yang Theory gives us the wisdom not to react in a one-sided fashion to a visible phenomenon or circumstance. You may get a promotion at work, which is great (Yang), but you may become busier and have less time to do things you like (Yin). You may be sad after ending a long-term relationship (Yin), but that may lead you to meet new people and find a better match eventually (Yang). If we see things in dual dimensions with Yin Yang Theory, we can stay calm and have peace whether we are experiencing Yin or Yang. While we may try to stay positive most of the time, negative thoughts will inevitably come up. But with this mindset, we do not need to fight those thoughts or deny them, but take their existence as the other side of "positive": After experiencing negative thoughts, soon positive thoughts will come back, and that is not good or bad. It is the way it is.

Feng Shui is an organic, holistic lifestyle. A healthy body encompasses a healthy mind, a healthy mind holds a healthy spirit, a healthy spirit exudes healthy energy, and good energy creates a positive environment. Living in such an environment is conducive to achieving your life goals. I believe that Feng Shui can be a strong tool for you to improve yourself, your relationships, and your lifestyle, while also improving your environment. I hope this book inspired you to start a holistic way of living—the Feng Shui lifestyle—and that, eventually, your positive energy will inspire other people, so that the good energy will flow all over the world.

APPENDIX

1. Add the last two numbers of your birth year and make it a single digit.

1981 → 8 + 1 = 9

2. Add the single digit to the number 5, and make that a single digit, too, if necessary.

9 + 5 = 14, then 1 + 4 = 5

Your Kua Number is 5! Your Five Element is Earth, and you are in West Group.

(For females born after the year 2000, add 6 instead of 5.)

HOW TO CALCULATE KUA NUMBER FOR MALES (BORN BEFORE THE YEAR 2000):

1. Add the last two numbers of your year of birth and make it a single digit.

1981 → 8 + 1 = 9

2. Deduct the single digit from the number 10. (For males born after the year 2000, subtract the single digit from 9 instead of 10.)

$$10 - 9 = 1$$

Your Kua Number is 1! Your Five Element is Water, and you are in East Group.

*KUA NUMBERS 1, 3, 4, 9 = EAST GROUP

1. Water
3. Wood / Thunder
4. Wood / Wind
9. Fire

*KUA NUMBERS 2, 5, 6, 7, 8 = WEST GROUP

2. Earth
5. Earth
6. Metal / Heaven
7. Metal / Lake
8. Earth / Mountain

INDEX

ABOUT THE AUTHOR

Ai Matsui Johnson is the owner of Ai Feng Shui Interior Consulting. After receiving her certification as a Feng Shui interior coordinator and color therapist in Japan in 2006, she has practiced in both Japan and New York. She also teaches at the New York Institute of Art + Design. She lives in Brooklyn, New York. You can find her on Instagram and Facebook at @aifengshuiinterior.